CITY OF WONDERS

Your Coloring Journey

101 Beautiful magical city illustrations

Kami Moon

City of Wonders: Your Coloring Journey

In a world where imagination knows no bounds, there exists a magical domain beyond the confines of reality. Welcome to the "City of Wonders," a coloring book that beckons you to embark on an extraordinary journey into the heart of your dreams.

As you open the pages of this book, you'll find yourself transported to the most captivating destinations your mind can conceive. Each page reveals a wondrous city like no other, a place where the ordinary becomes extraordinary, and the mundane takes on a touch of magic.

Imagine strolling through "Ethereal Euphoria," a metropolis suspended in the sky, its buildings adorned with floating gardens and shimmering waterfalls. Or perhaps you'd prefer to explore "Luminous Labyrinth," a metropolis of crystalline structures that glow with a mesmerizing iridescence, nestled deep within an enchanted forest.

As you flip through the pages, you'll encounter "Dragon's Haven," a metropolis where majestic dragons roam freely, coexisting harmoniously with the inhabitants.

But the magic doesn't stop there. Within these pages, you are not just a spectator; you are the artist, the architect, and the magician. You hold the power to bring these enchanting metropolises to life with your colors, your imagination, and your unique vision.

With every stroke of your brush or pencil, you breathe life into these fantastical metropolises. Will the sky be cerulean blue or a fiery crimson at sunset? Are the trees adorned with emerald leaves, or do they shimmer with an otherworldly silver glow? It's your choice, your world to create.

"City of Wonders: Your Coloring Journey" is an invitation to embrace your inner artist, to escape the ordinary, and to rediscover the joy of coloring. It's a passport to a world of endless possibilities, where every stroke of color transforms the ordinary into the extraordinary.

Turn the first page, and let your adventure begin. Allow your colors to paint the story of the "City of Wonders," and let your heart be filled with the magic of creation. Join us on this remarkable journey through the land of fantasy, where every stroke of color is a step closer to discovering the wonders of your own imagination.

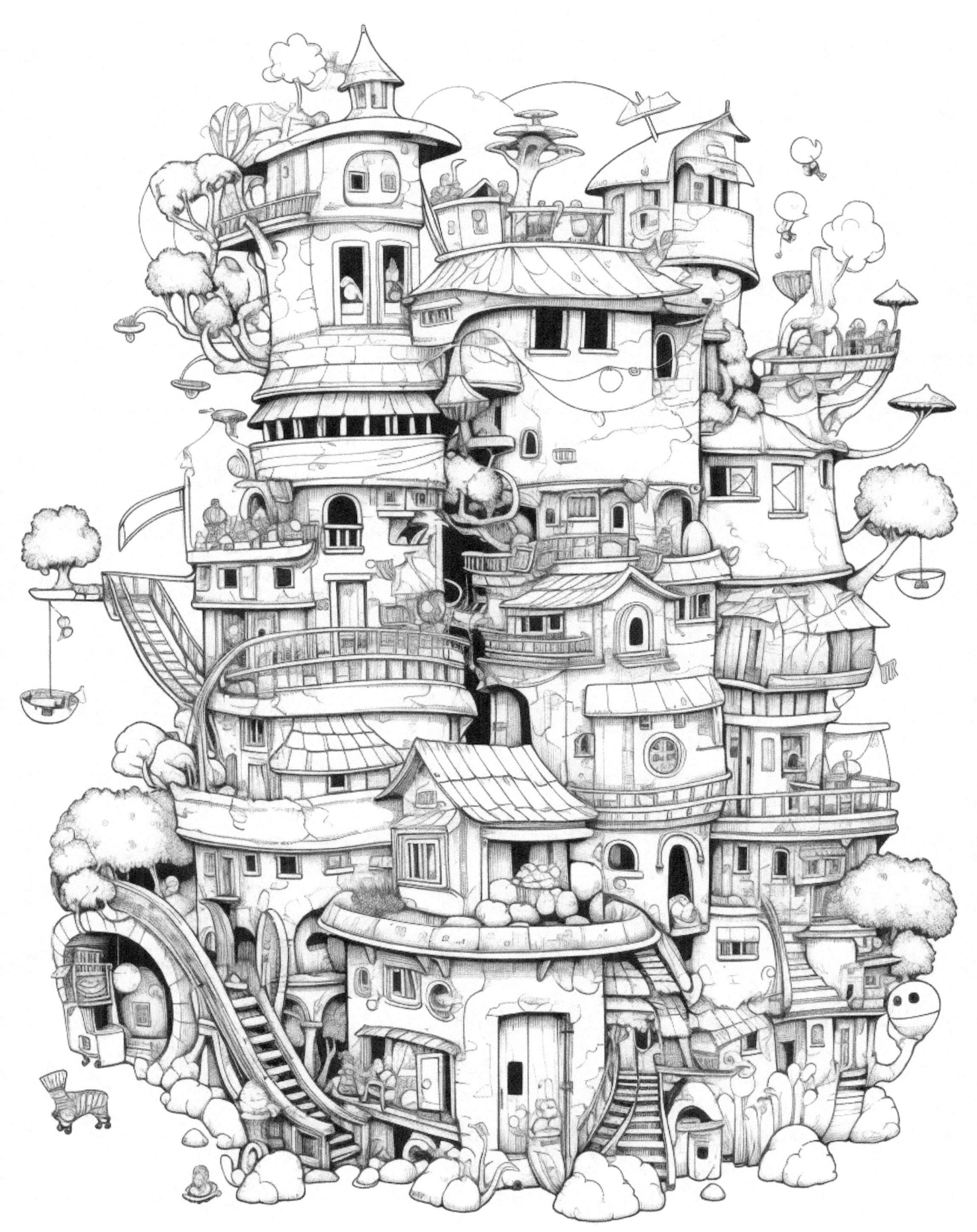

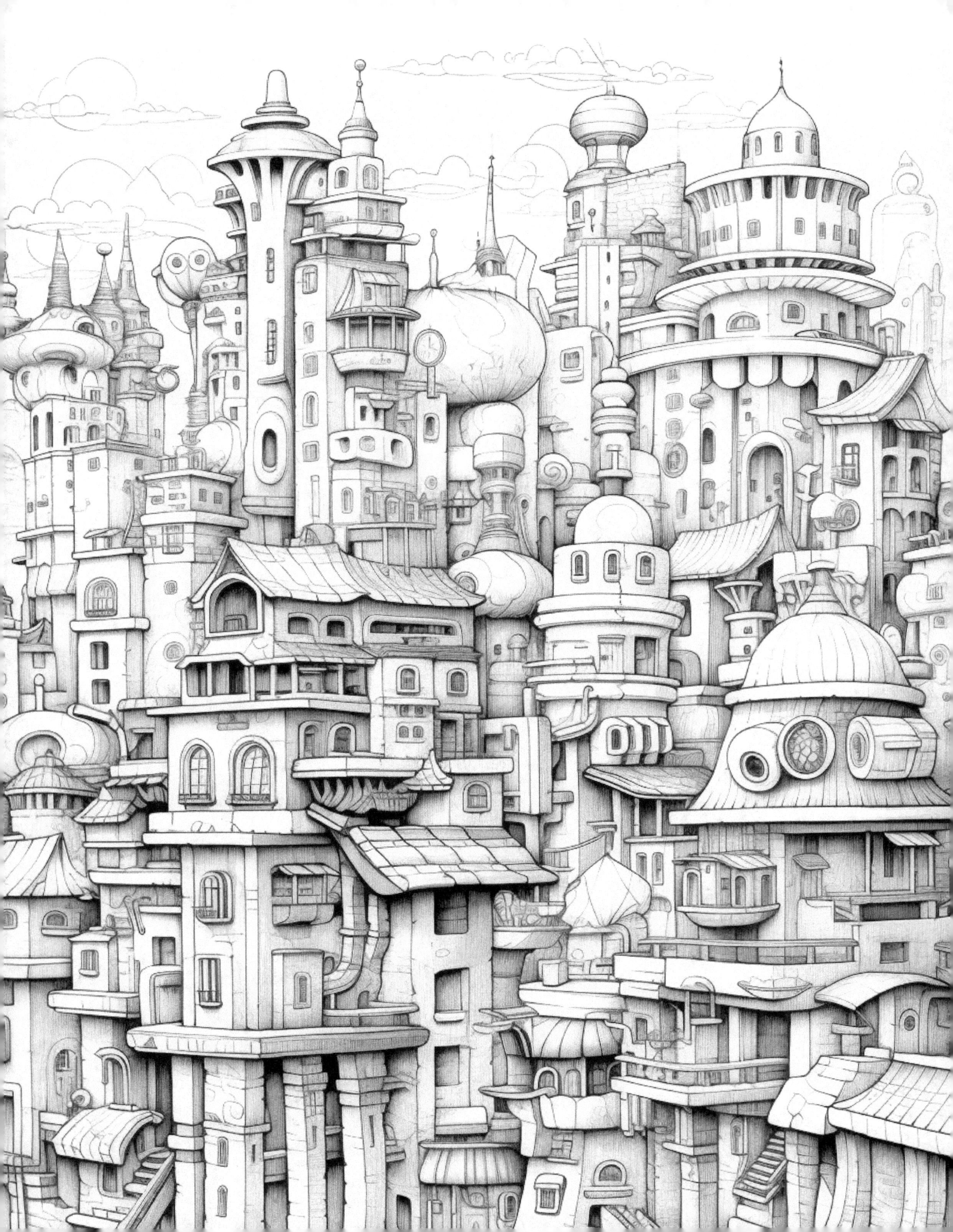

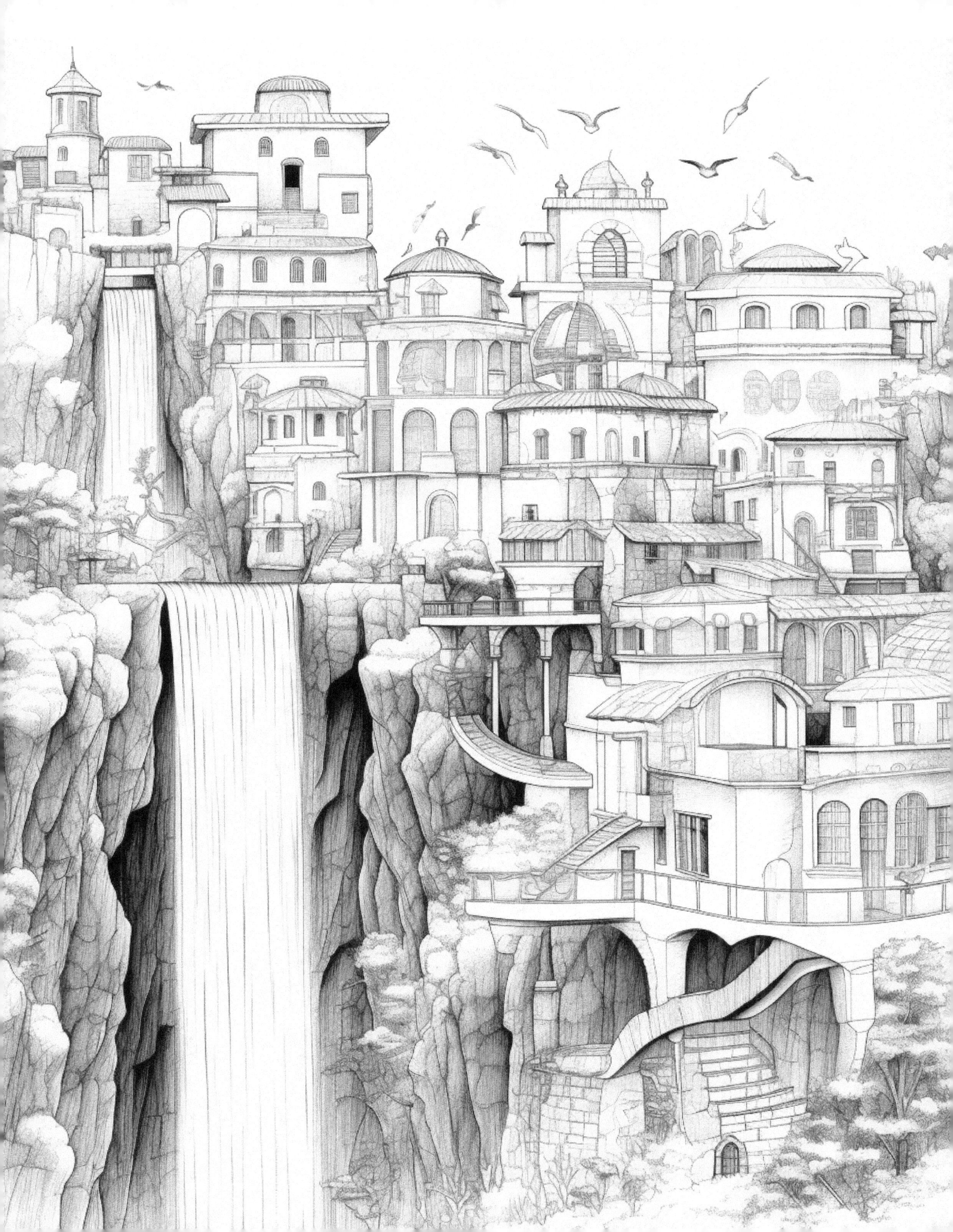

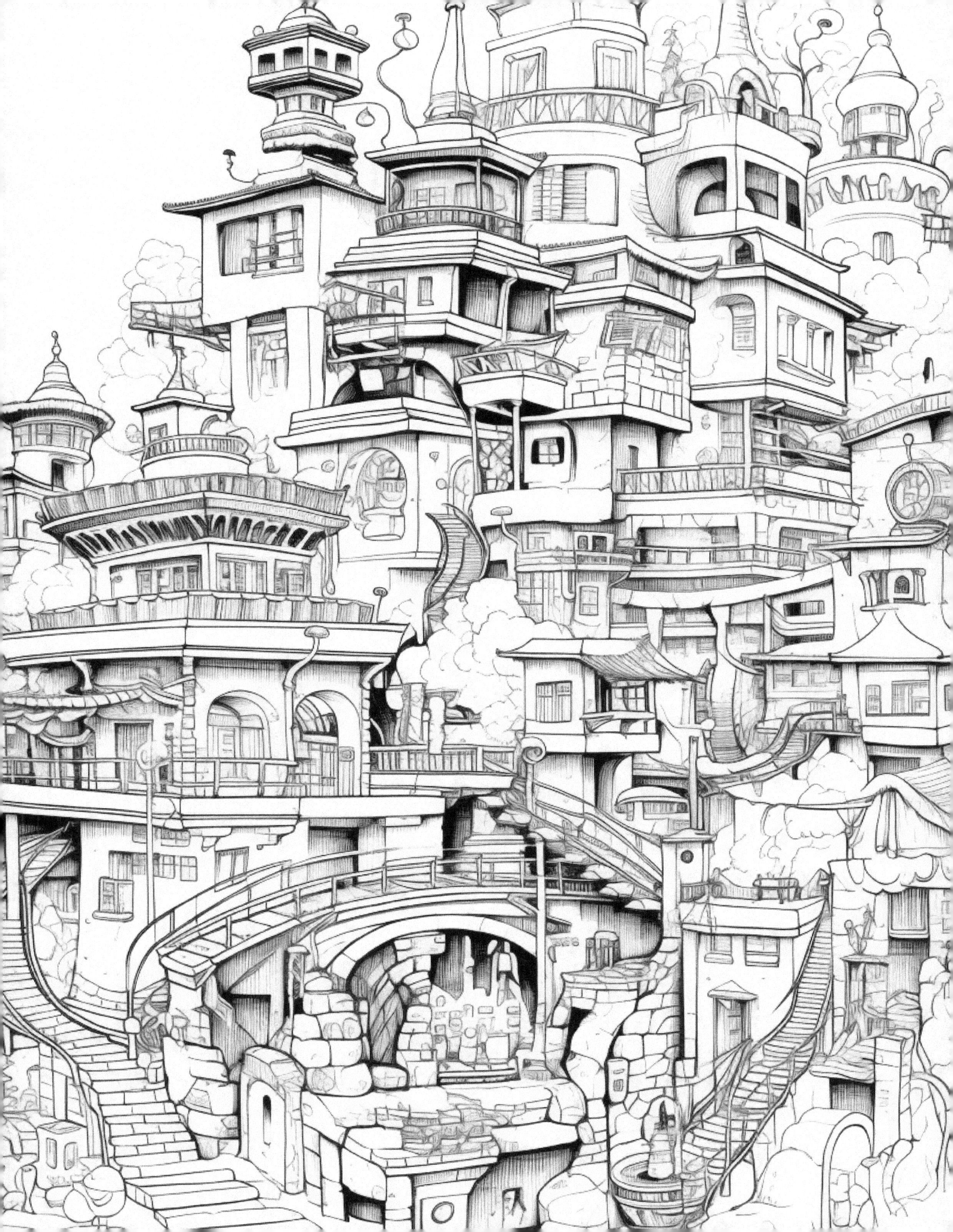

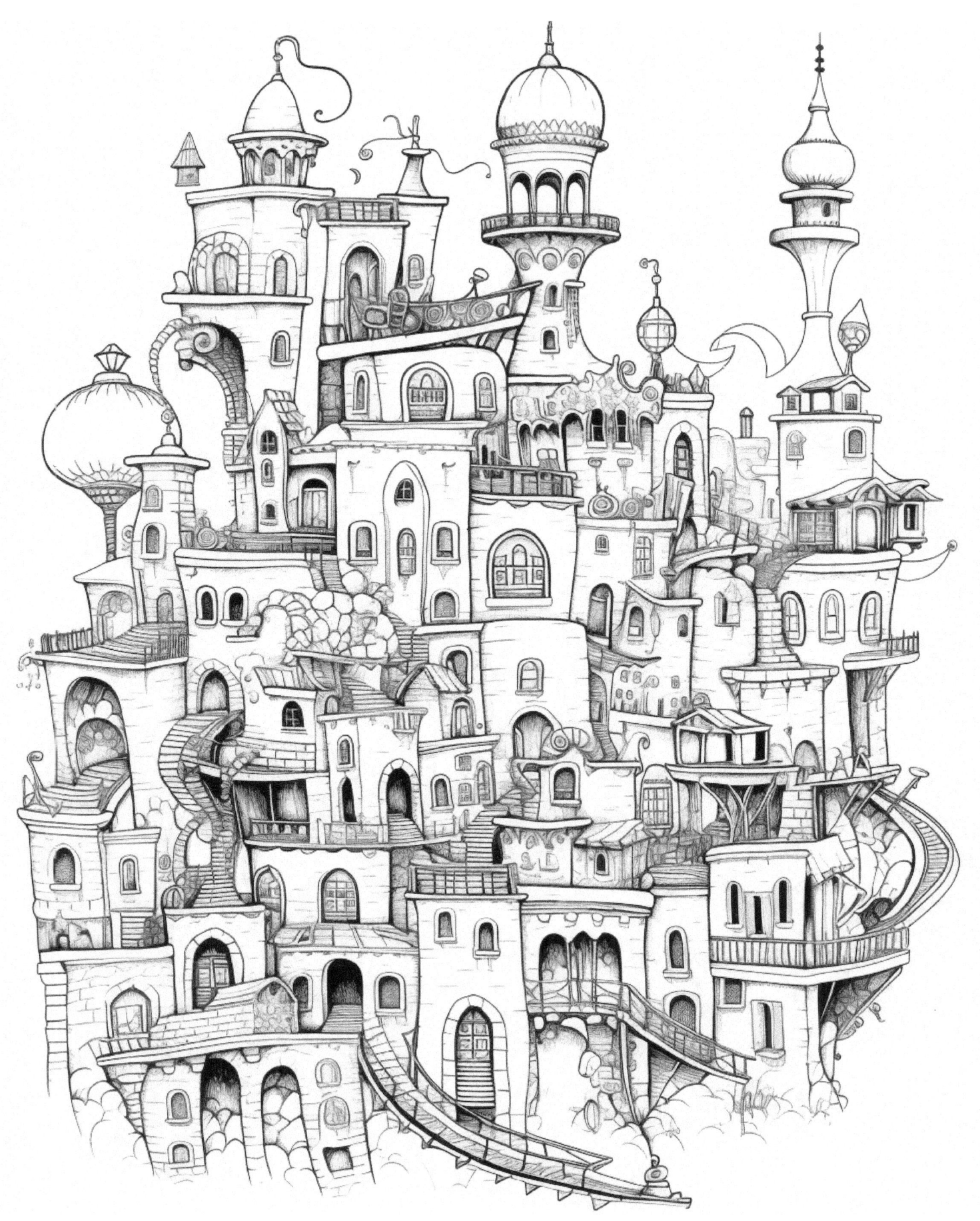

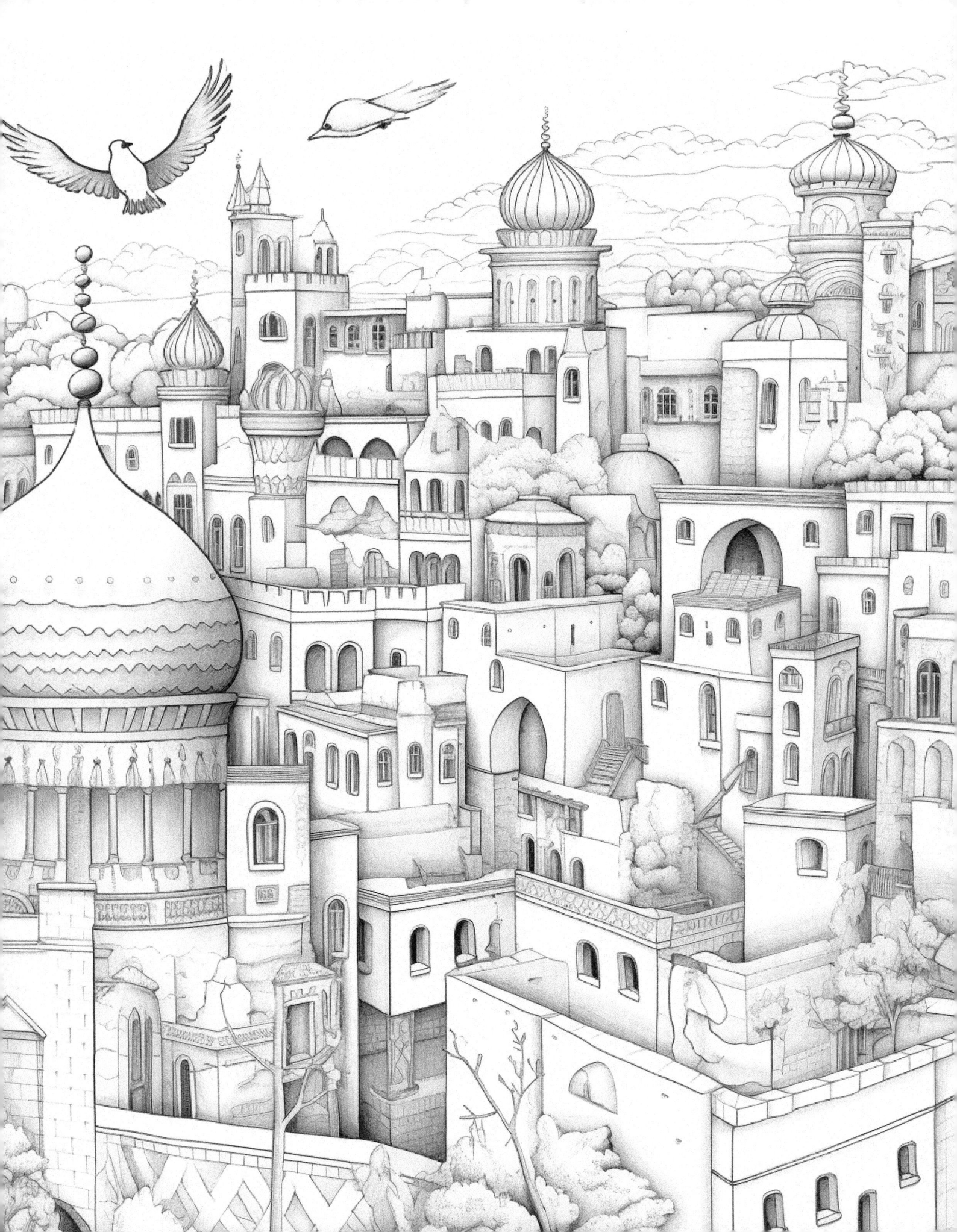

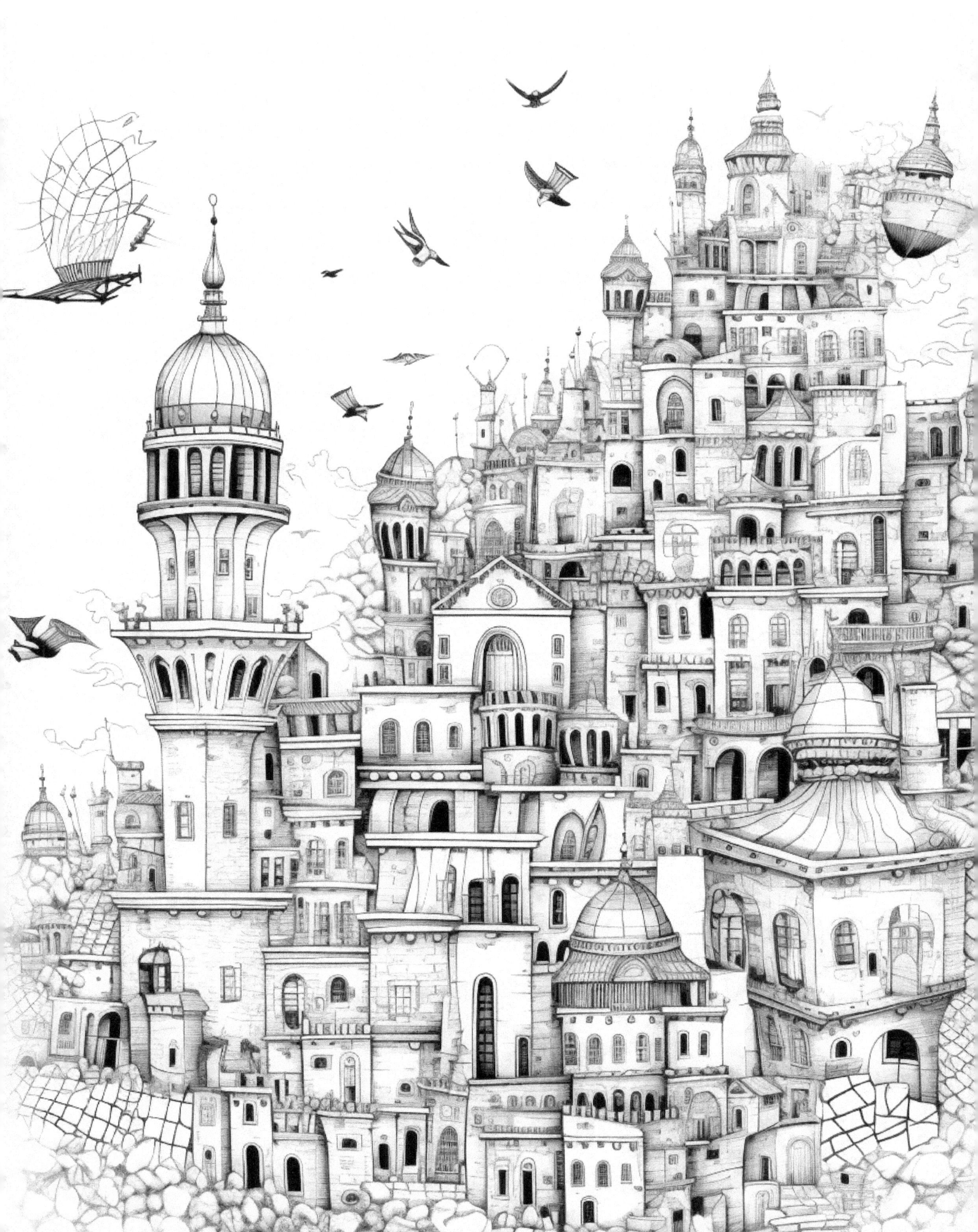

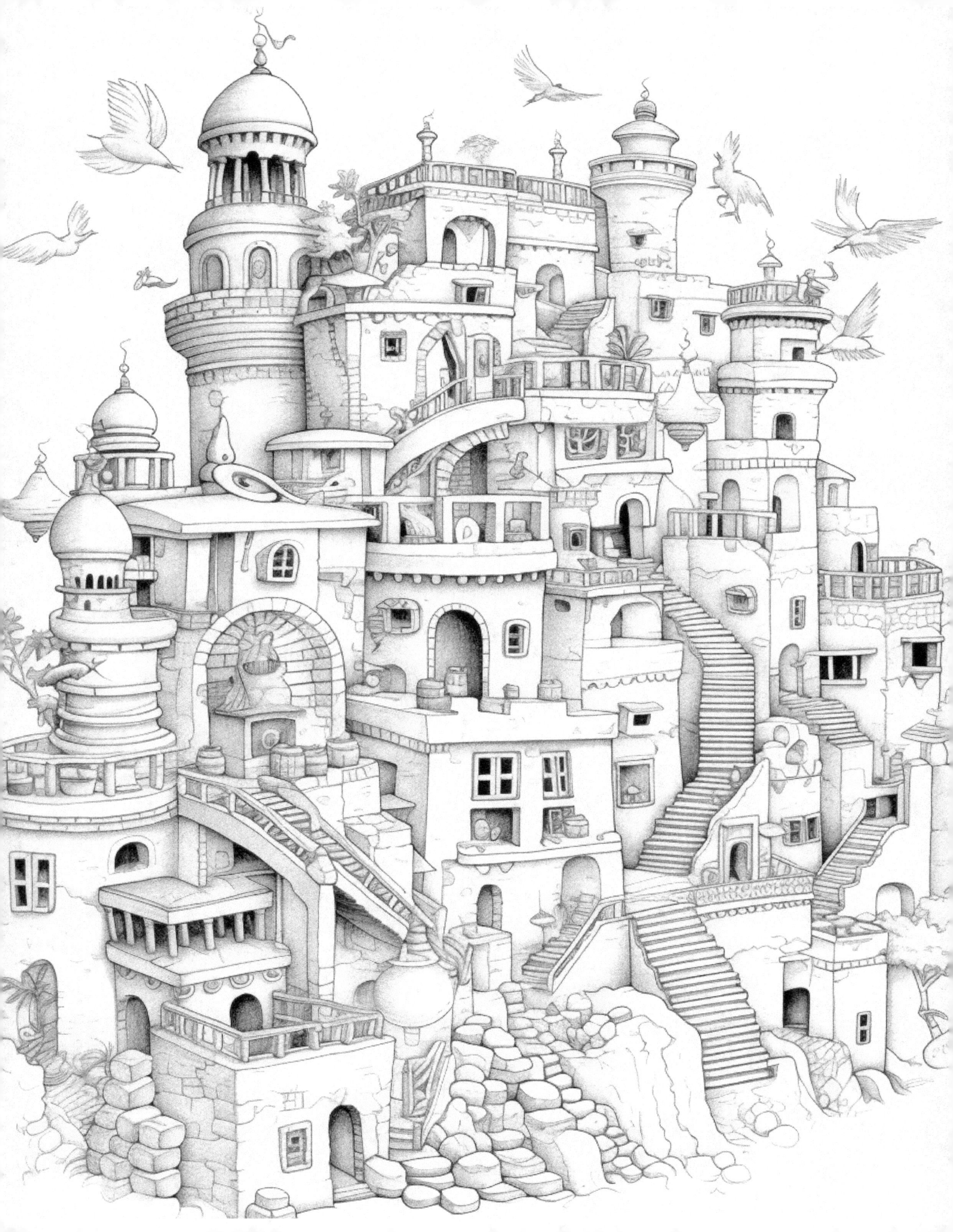

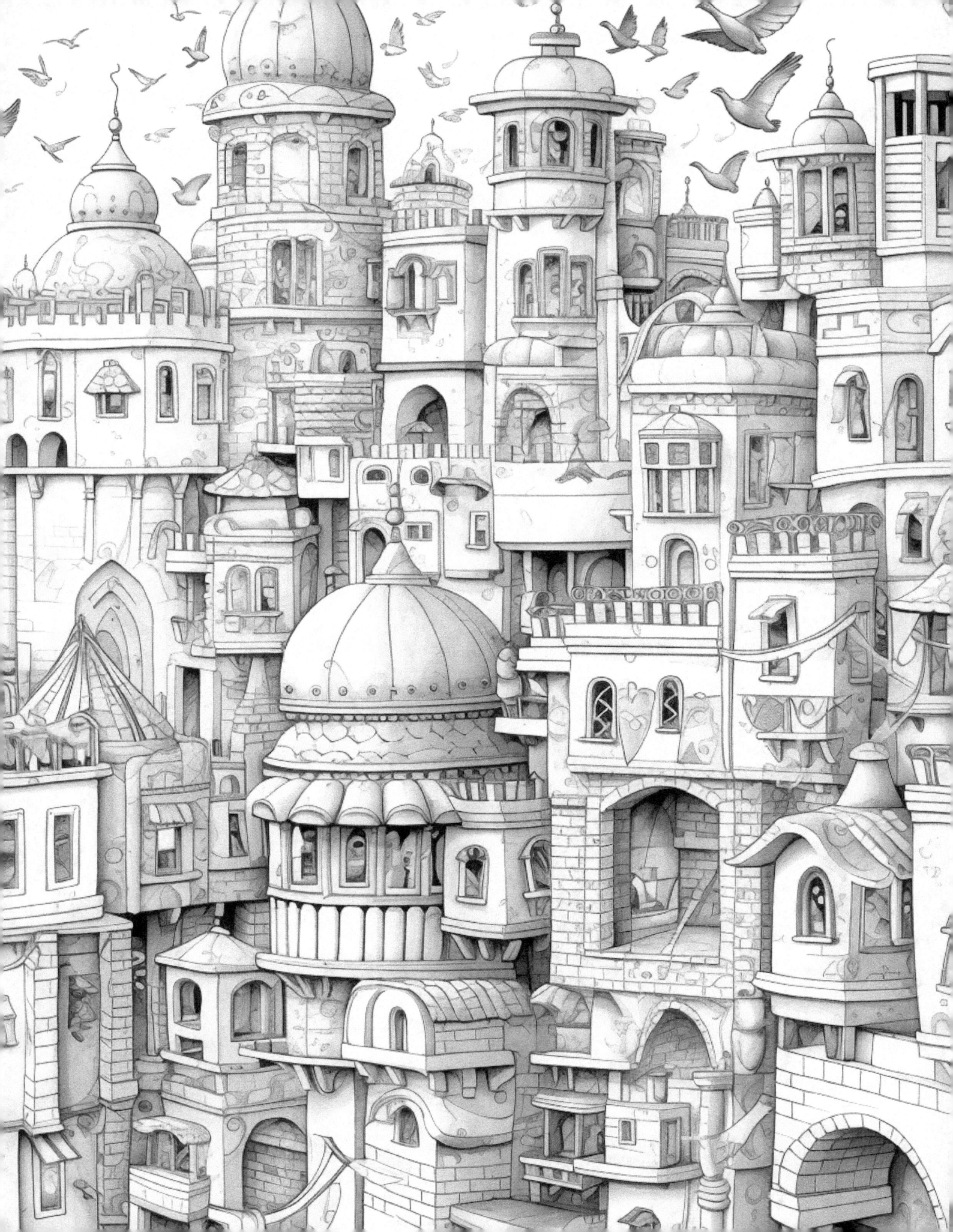

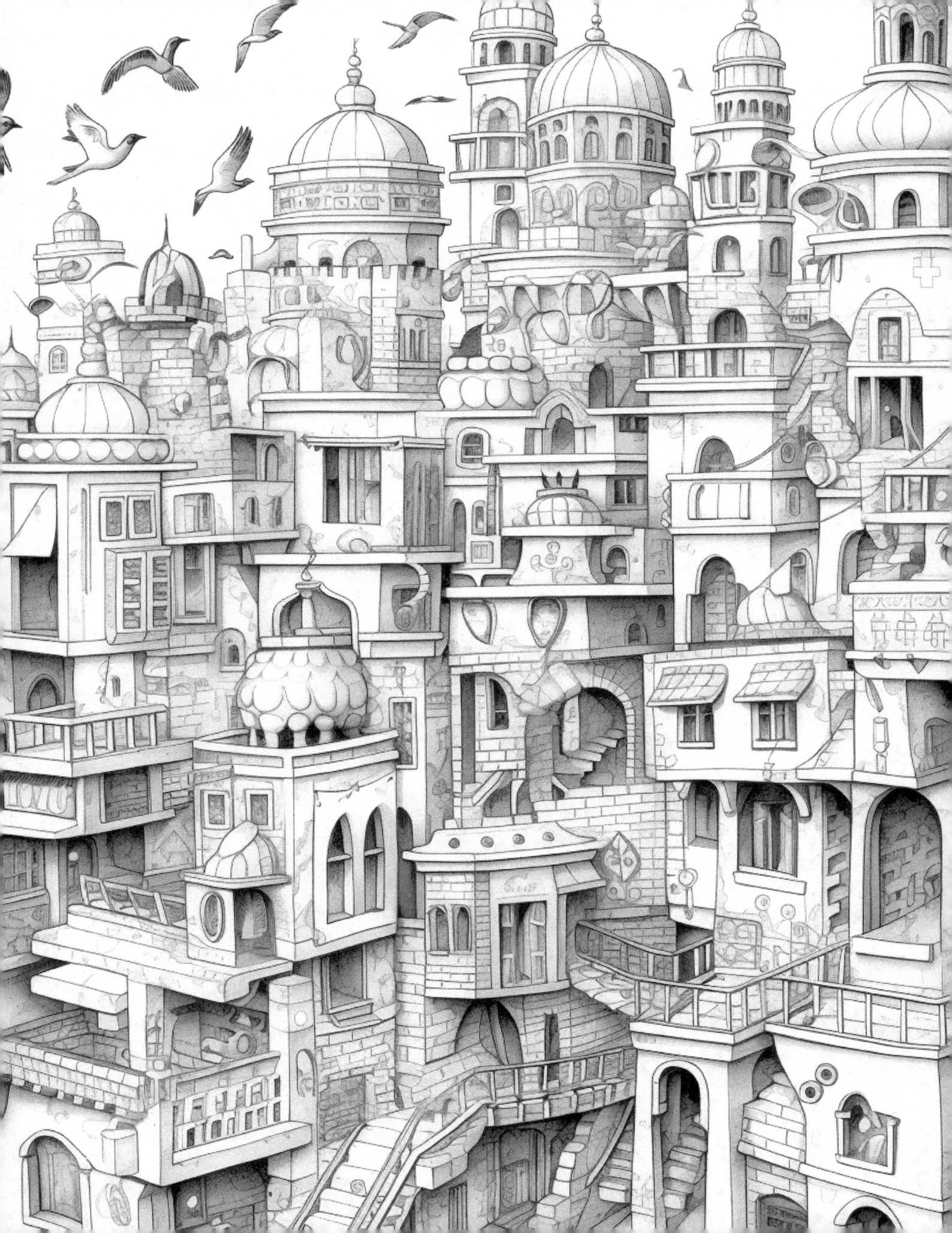

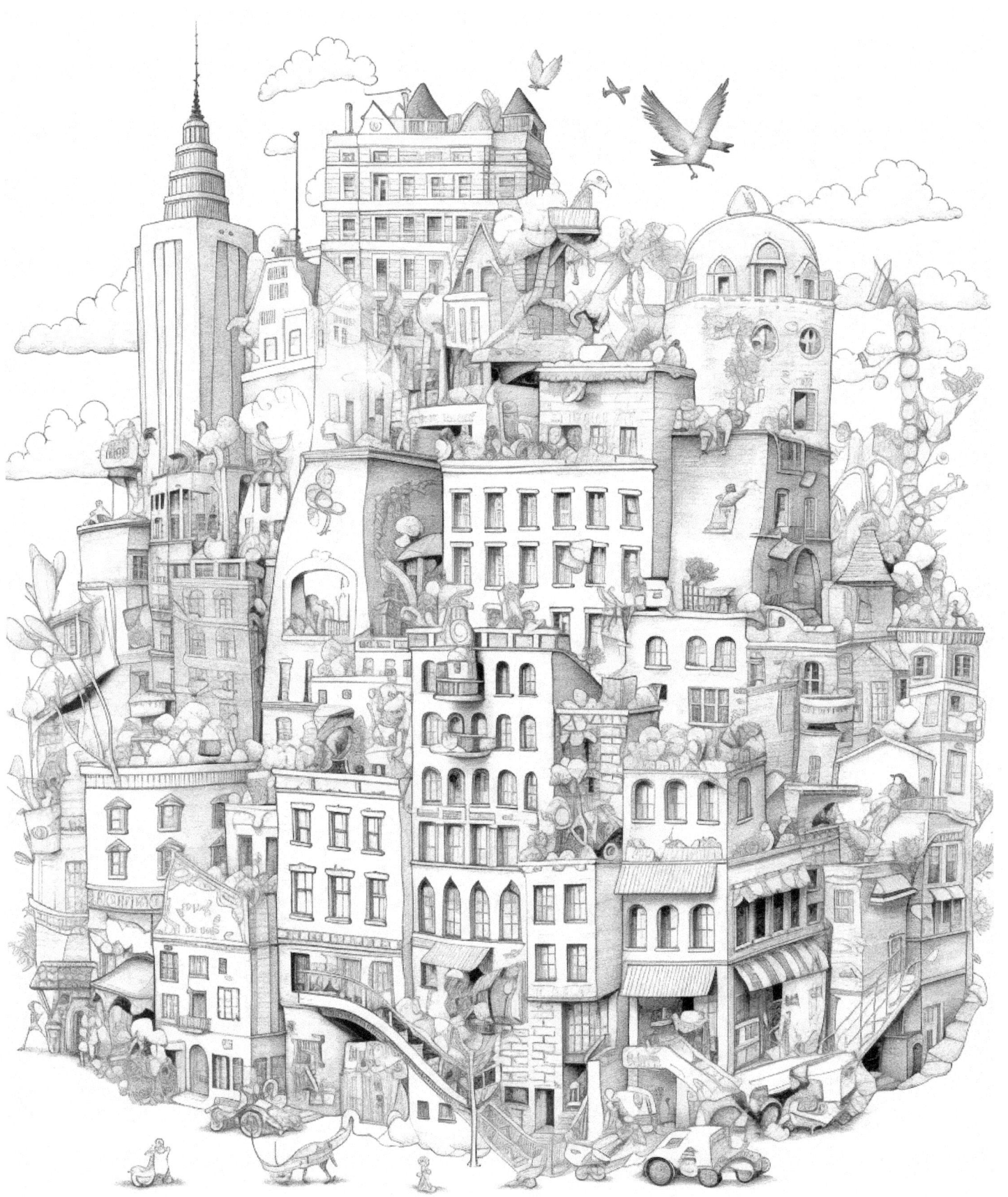

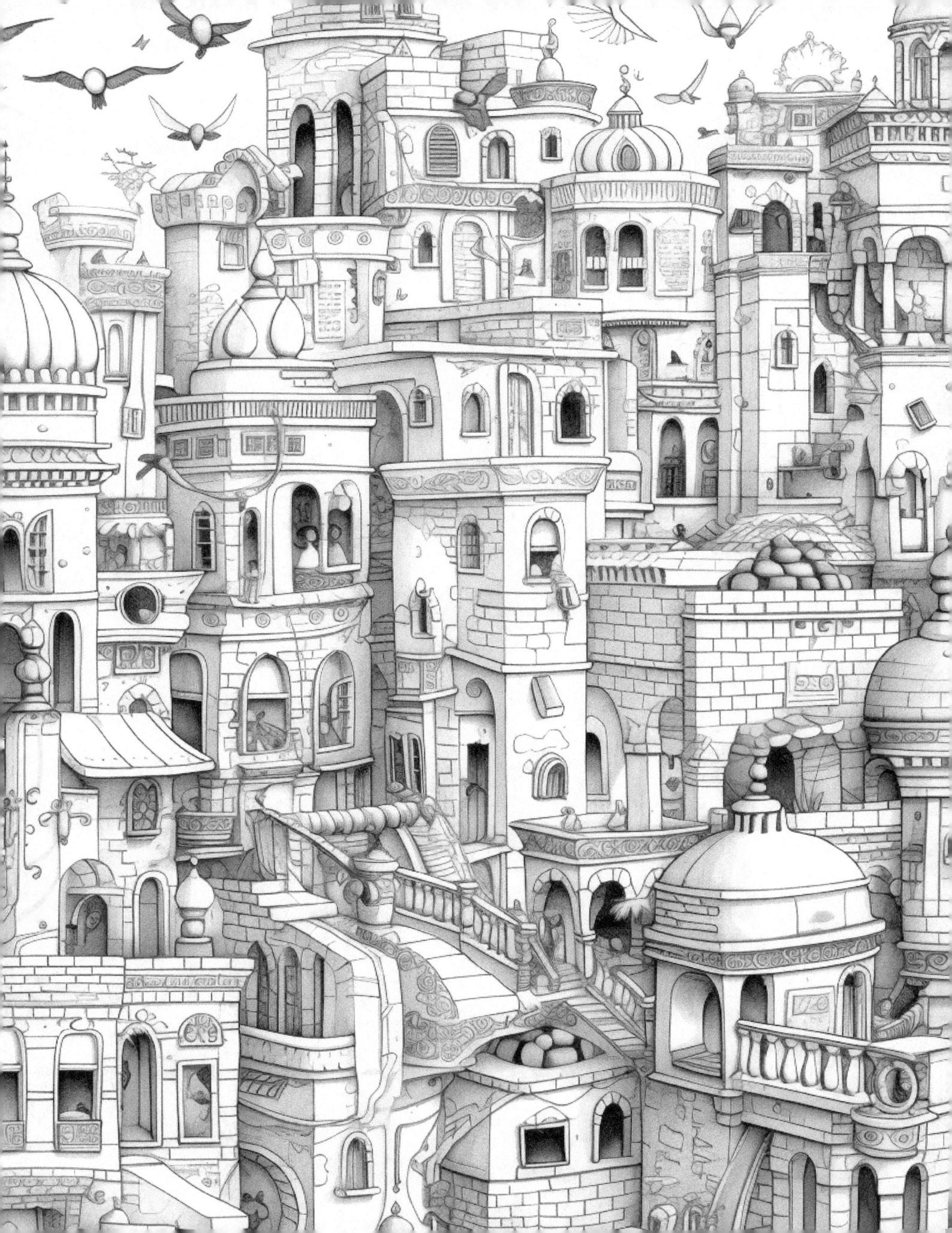

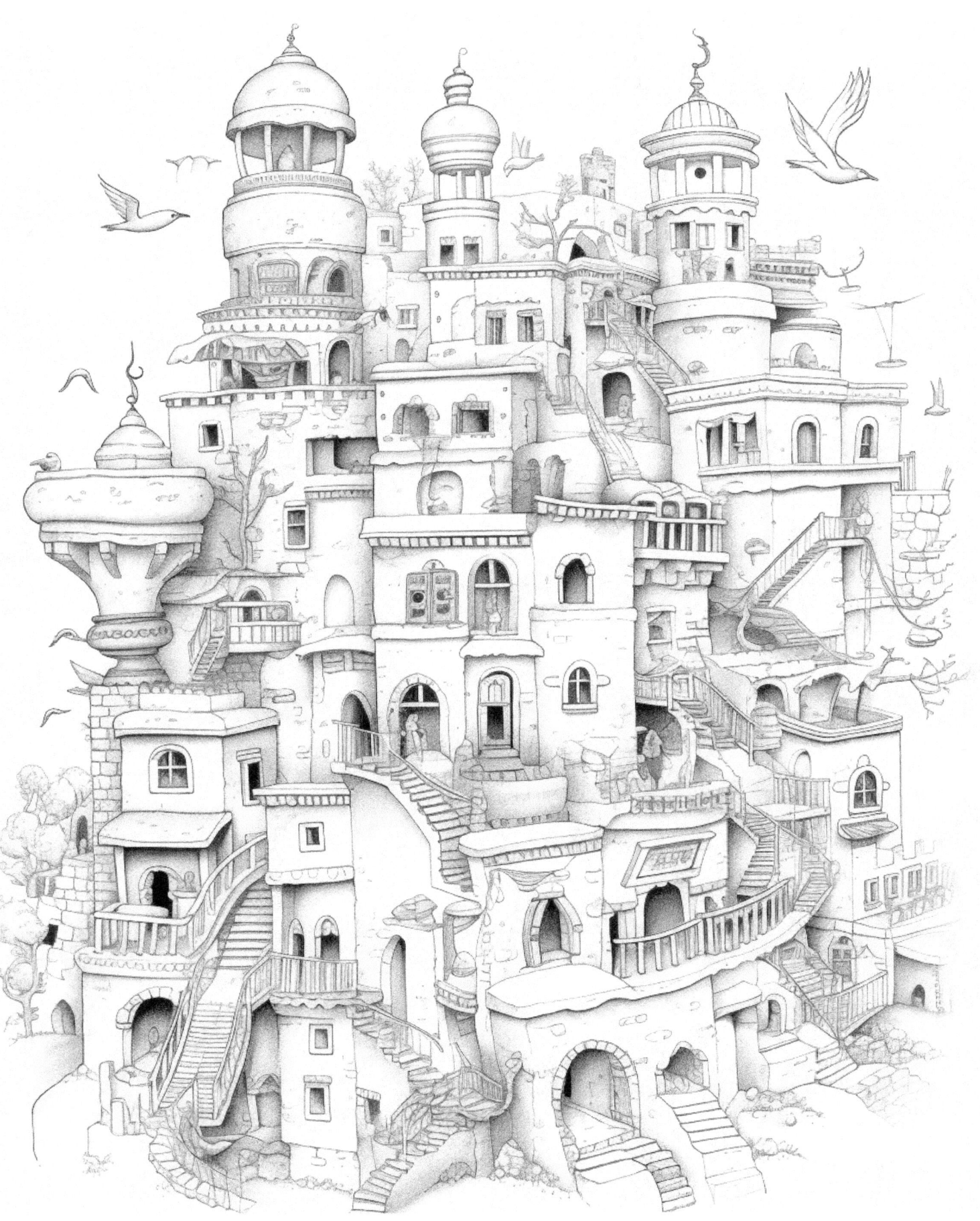

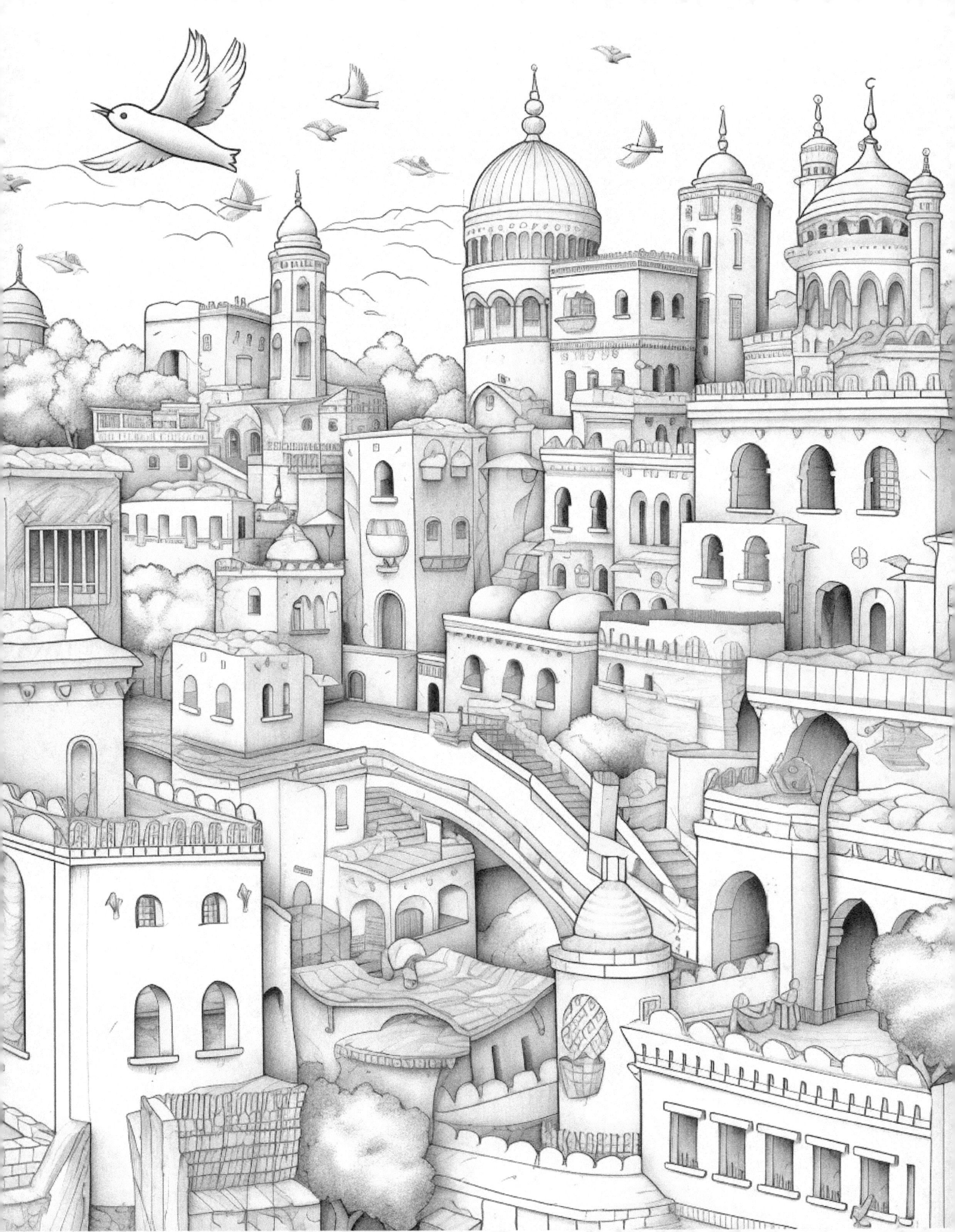

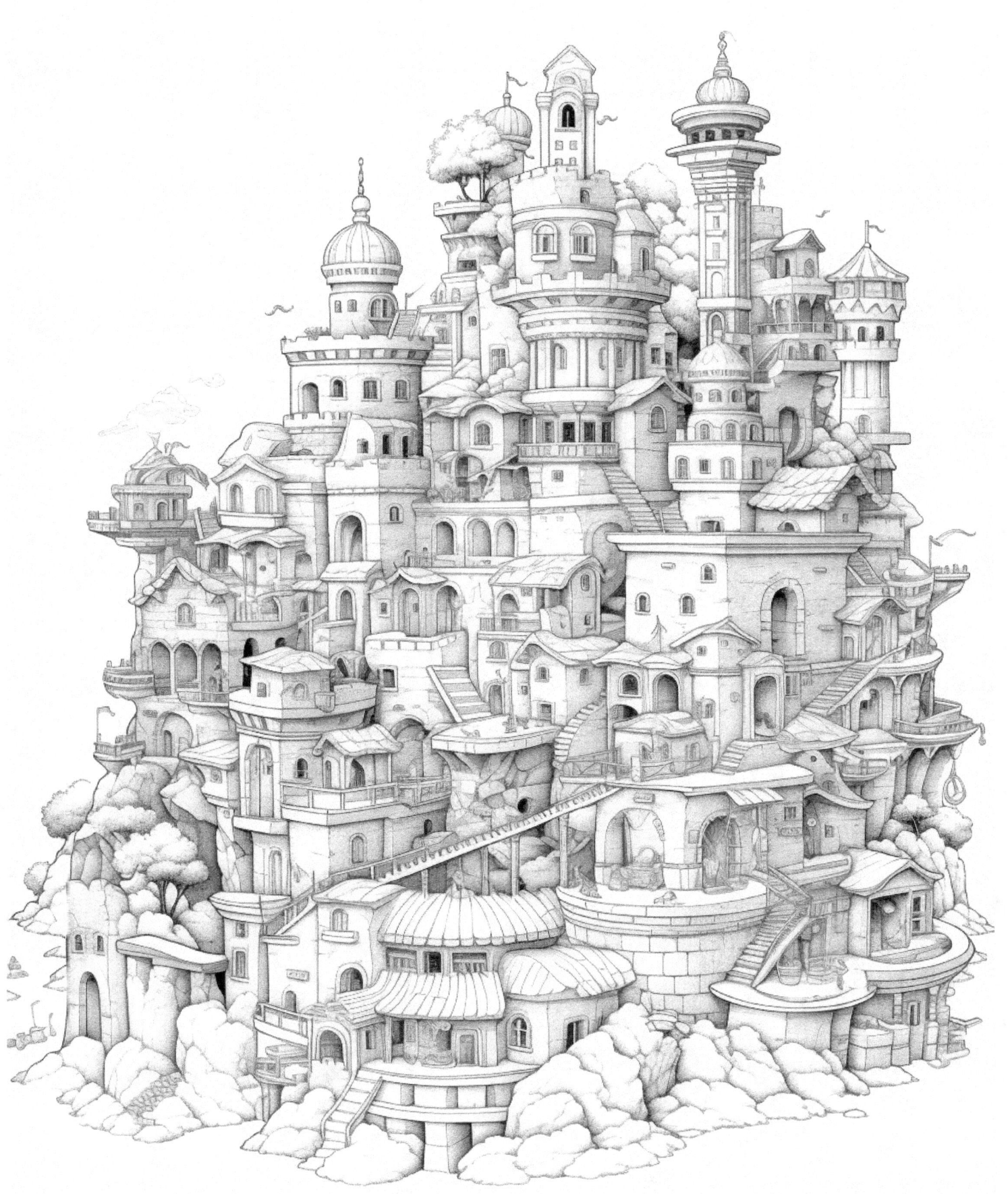

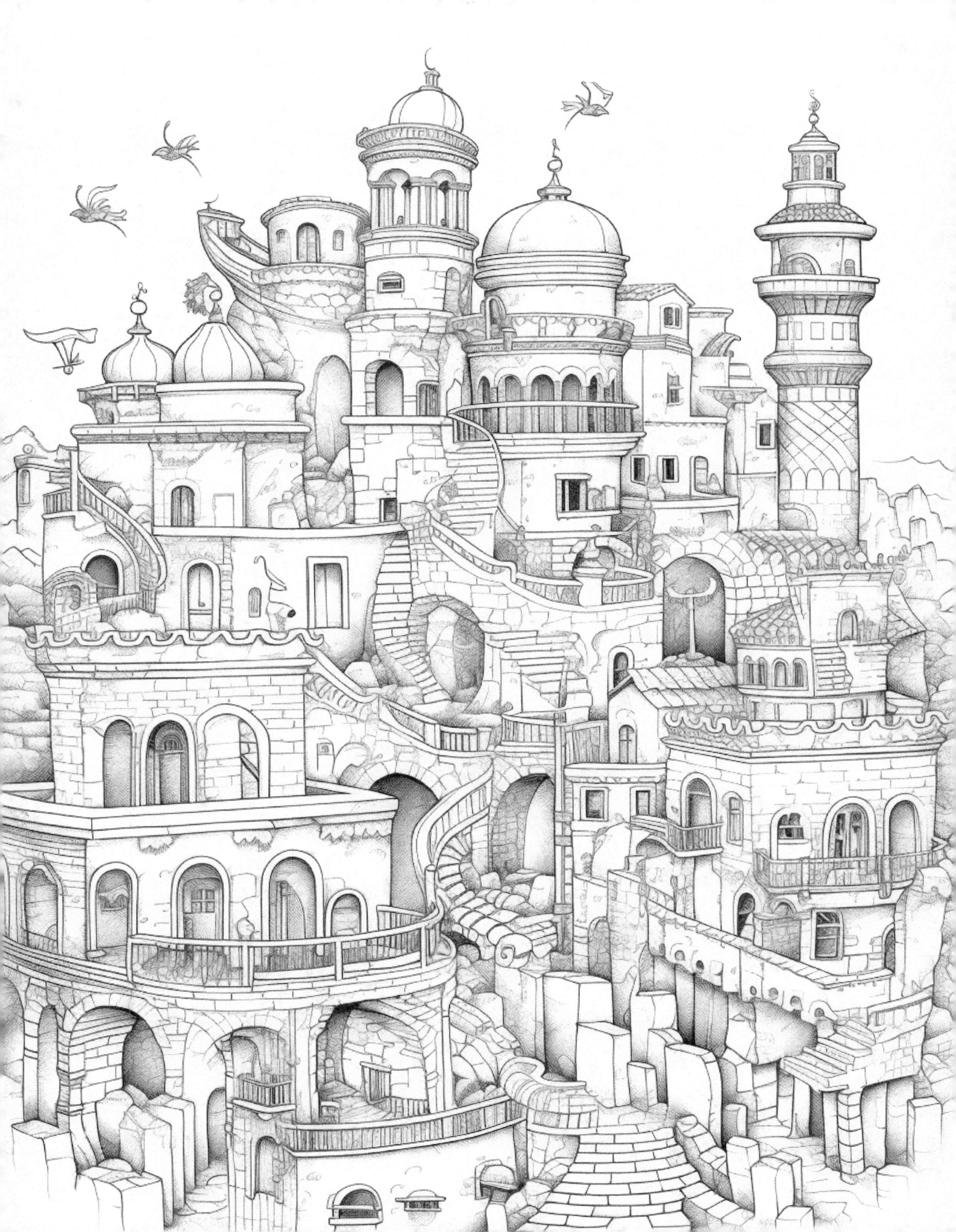

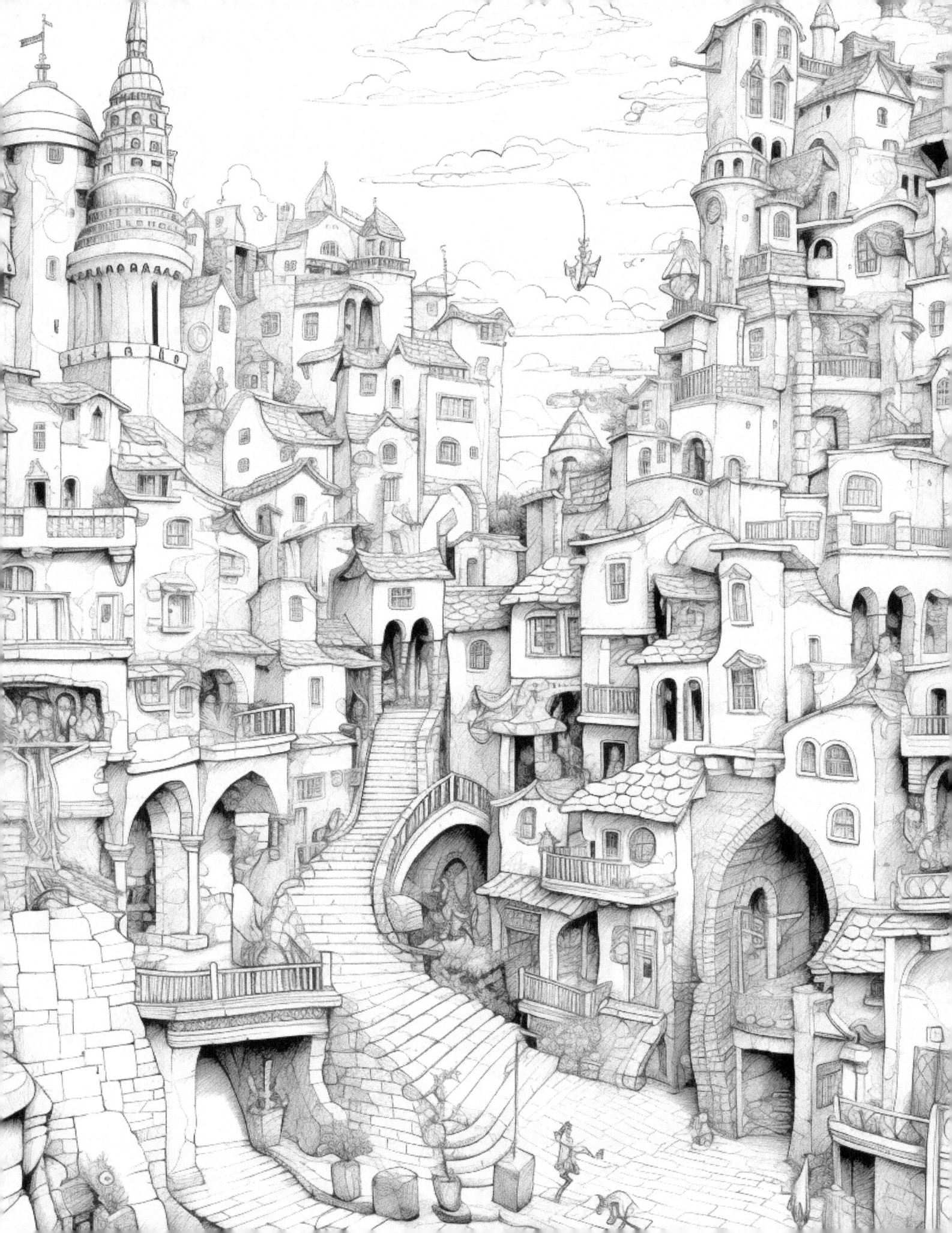

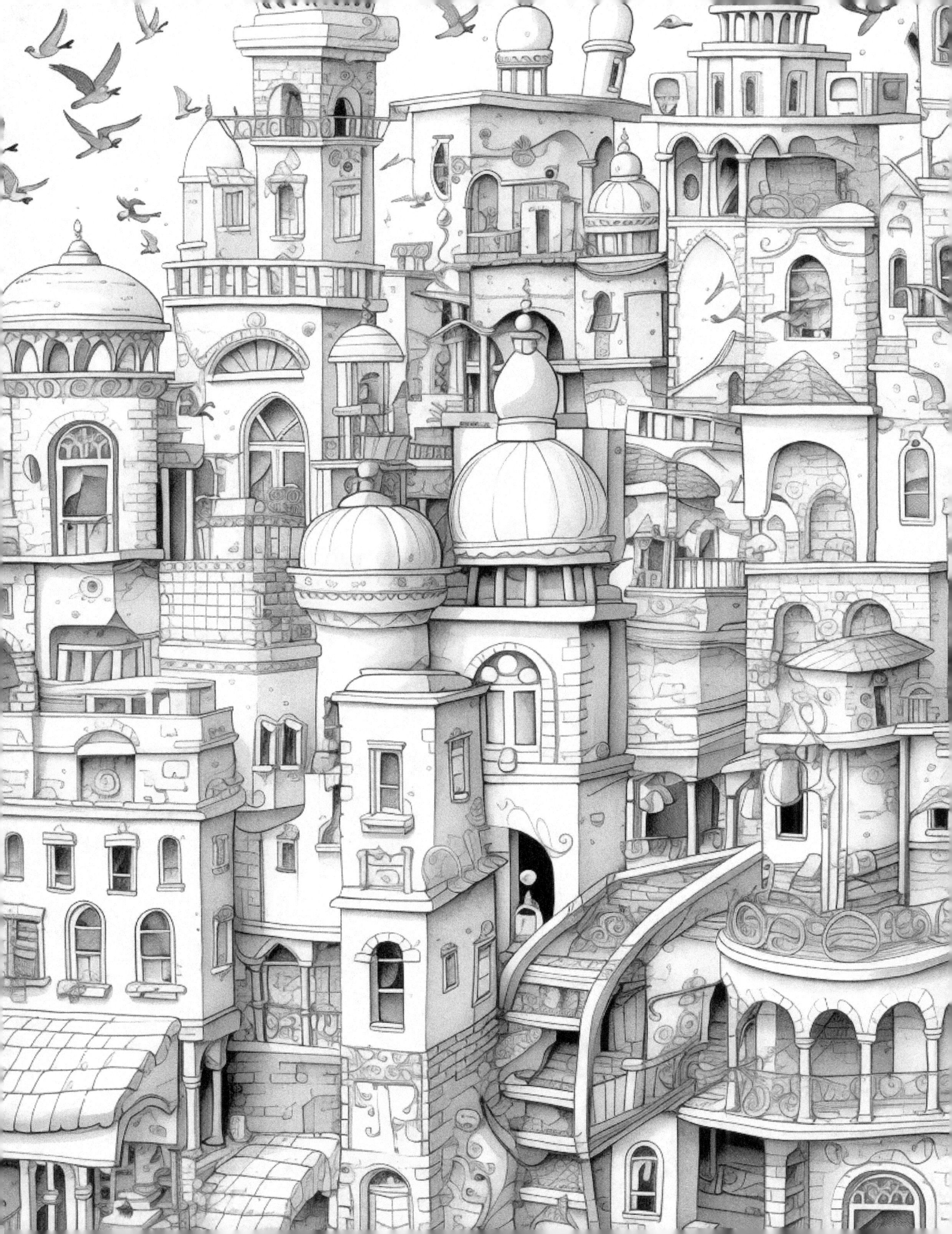

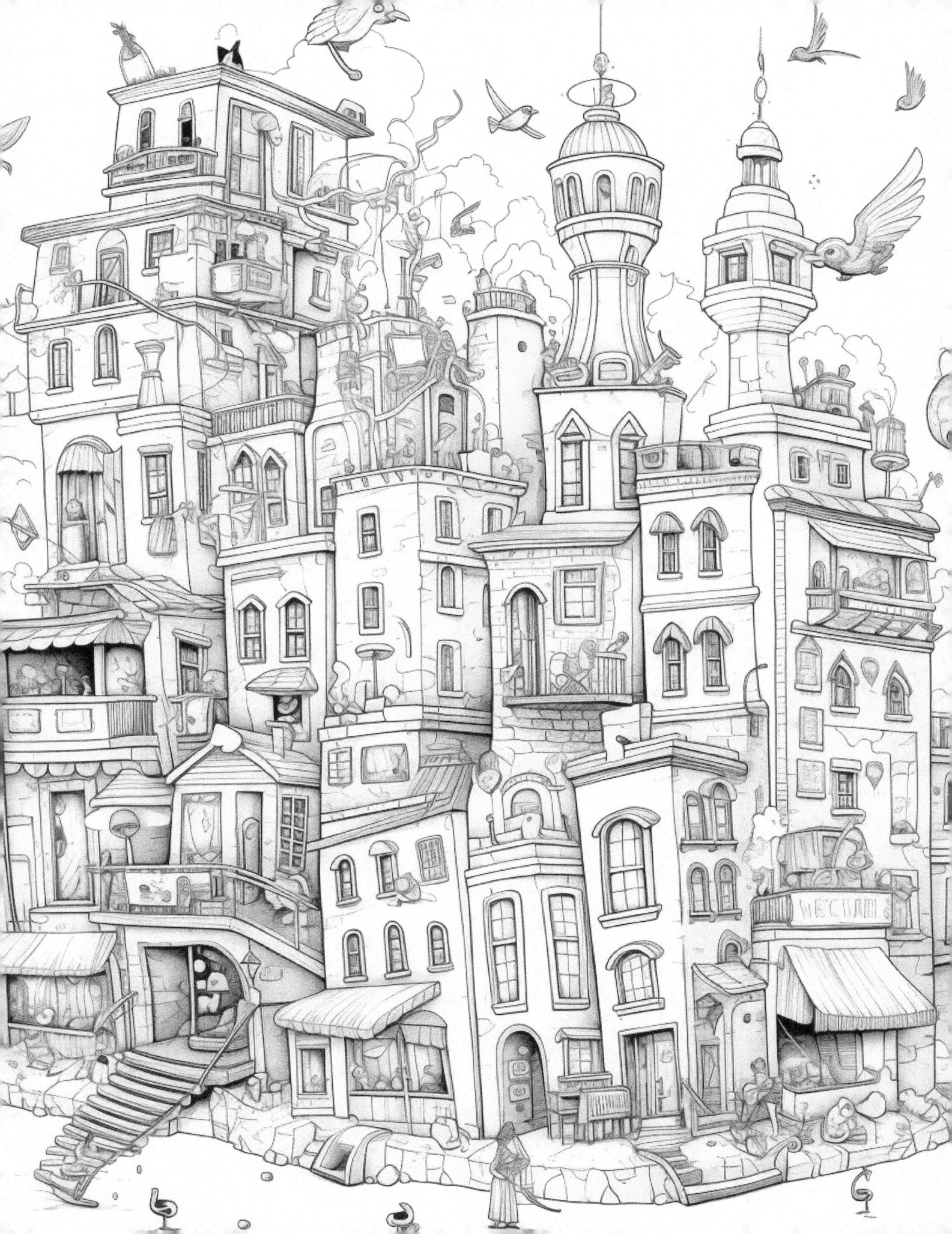

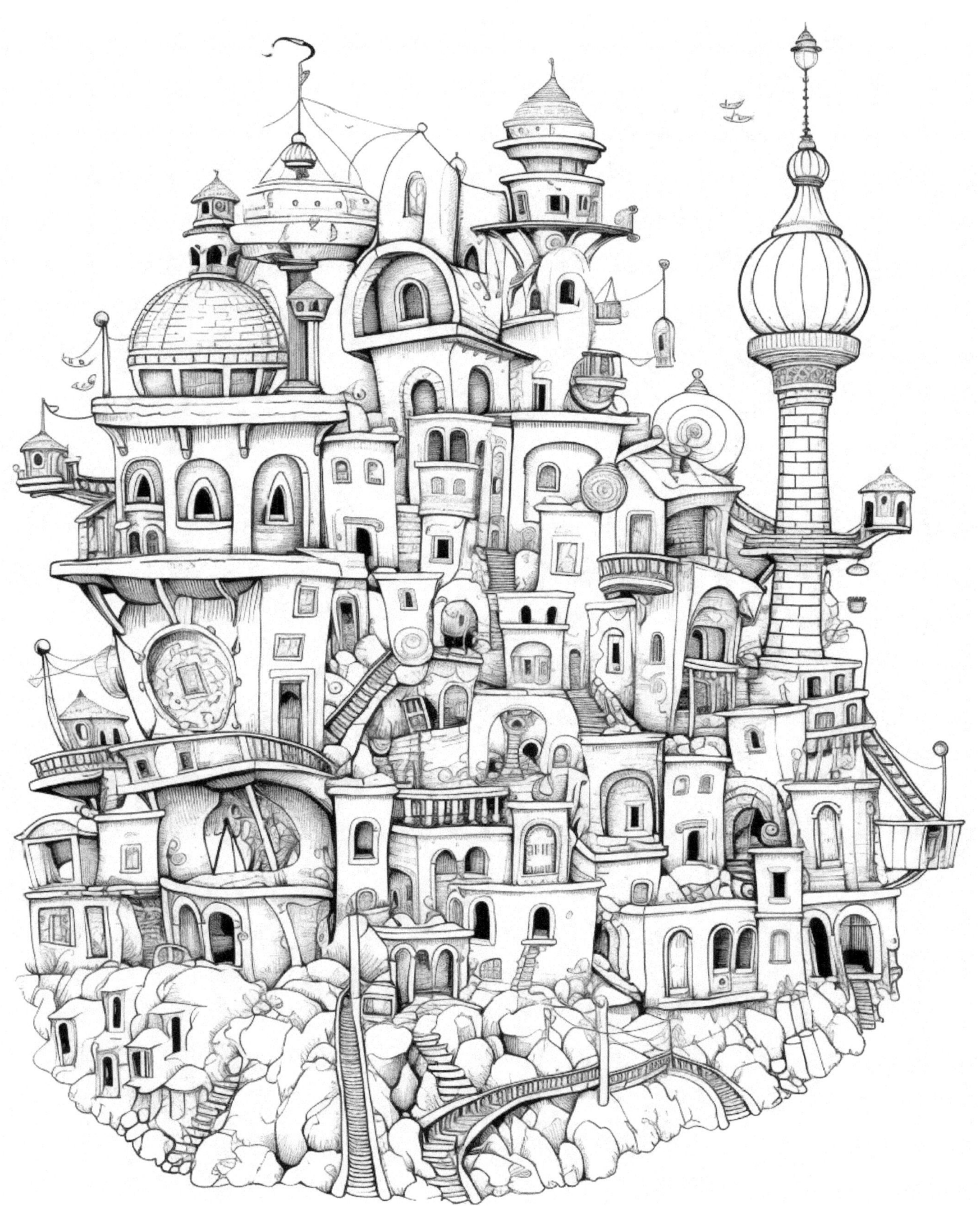

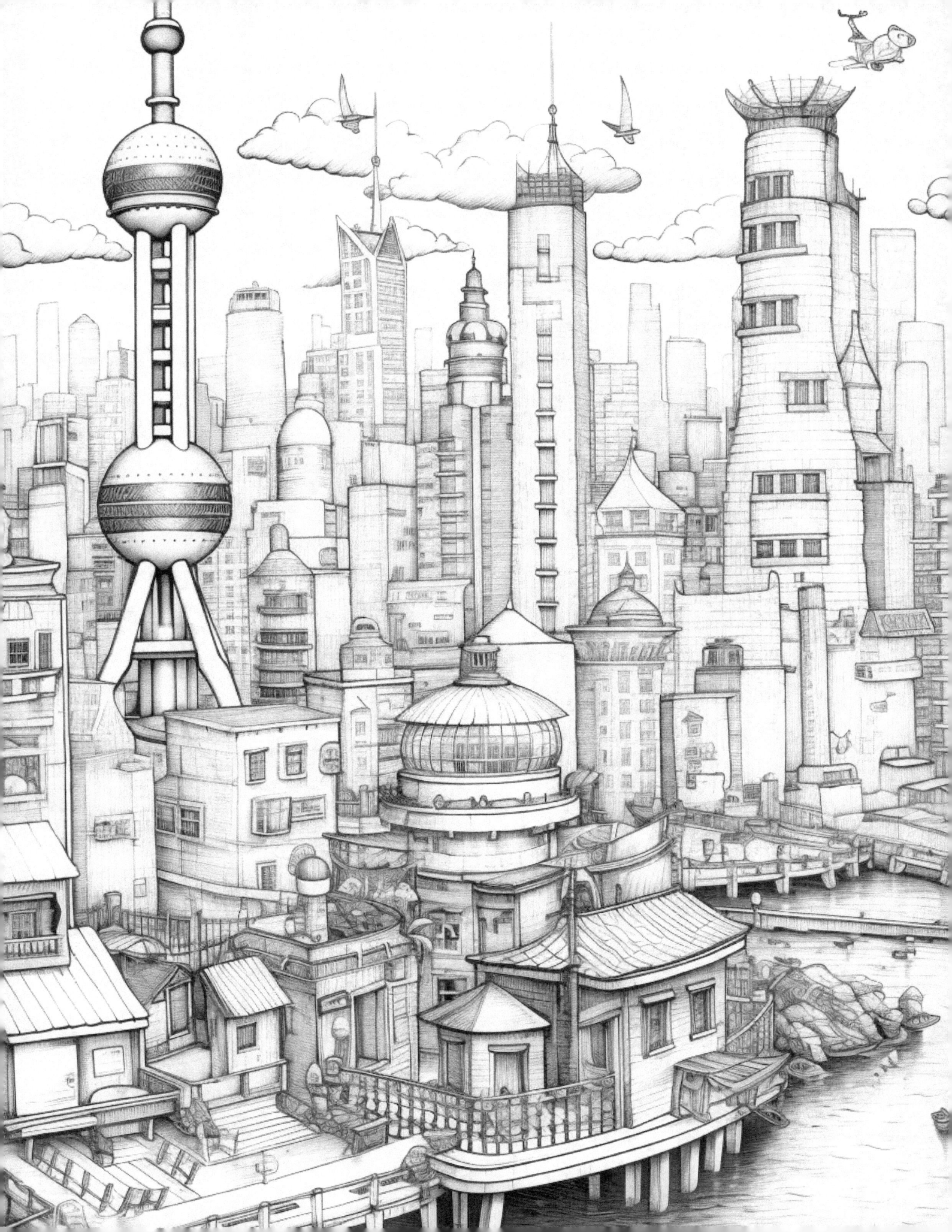

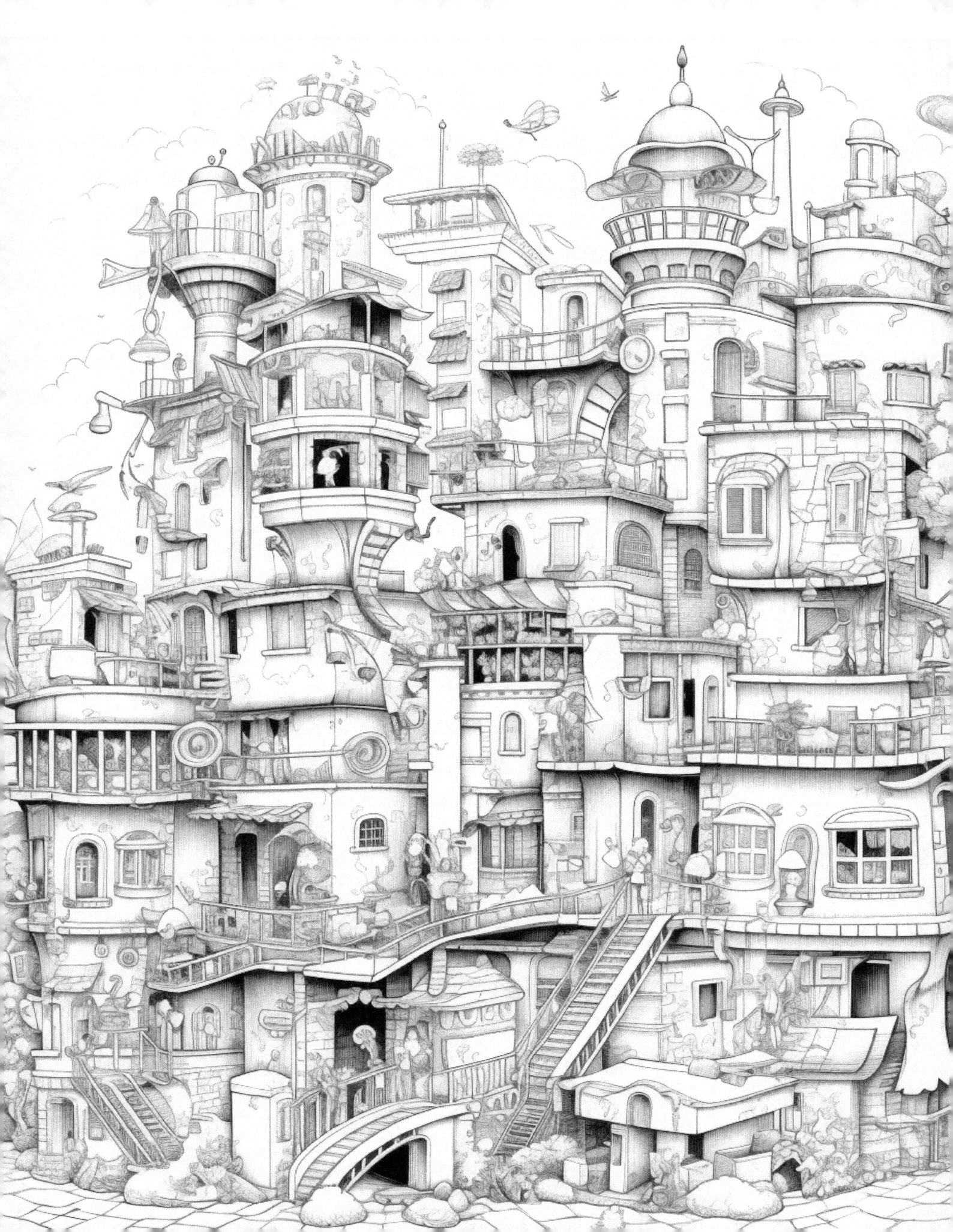

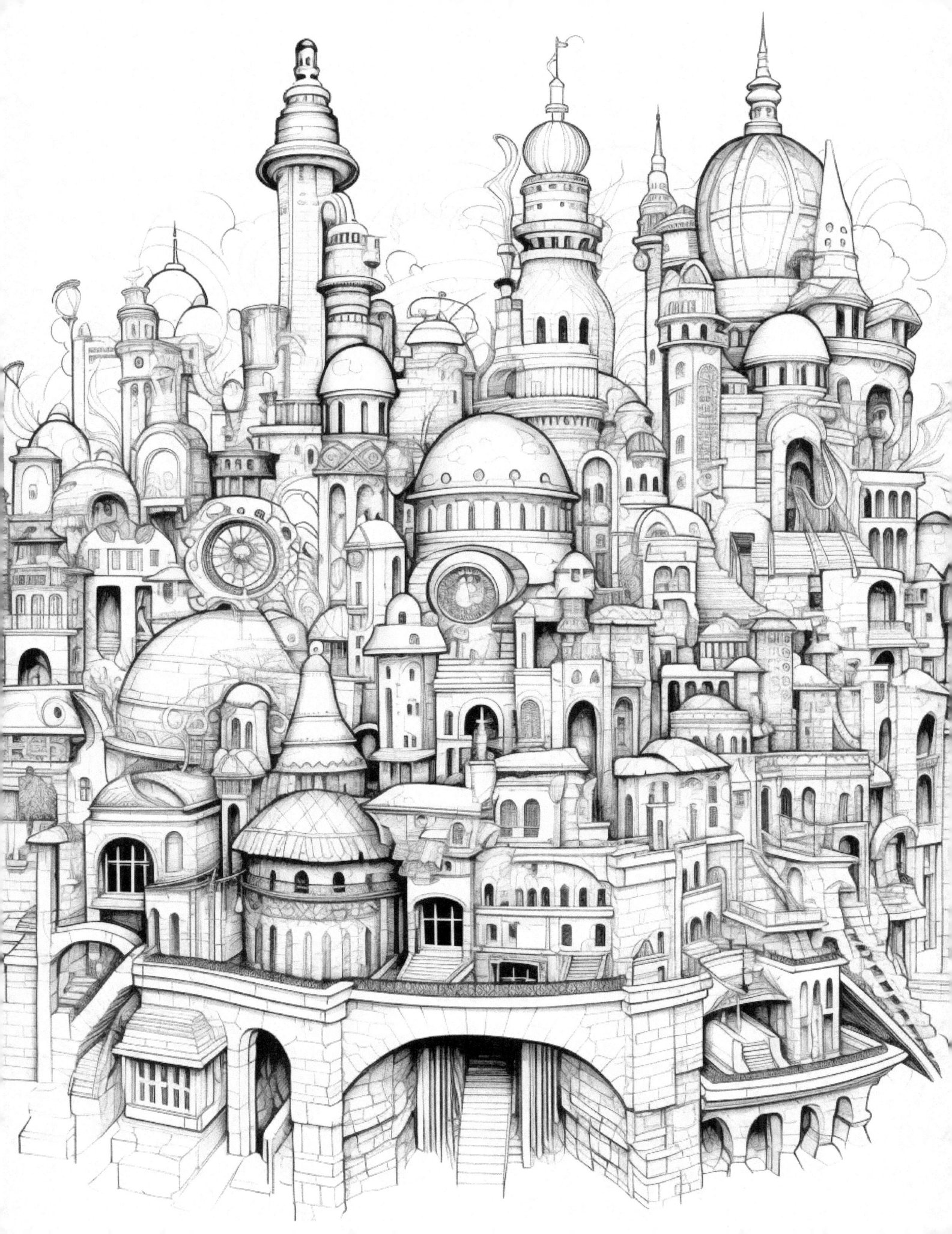

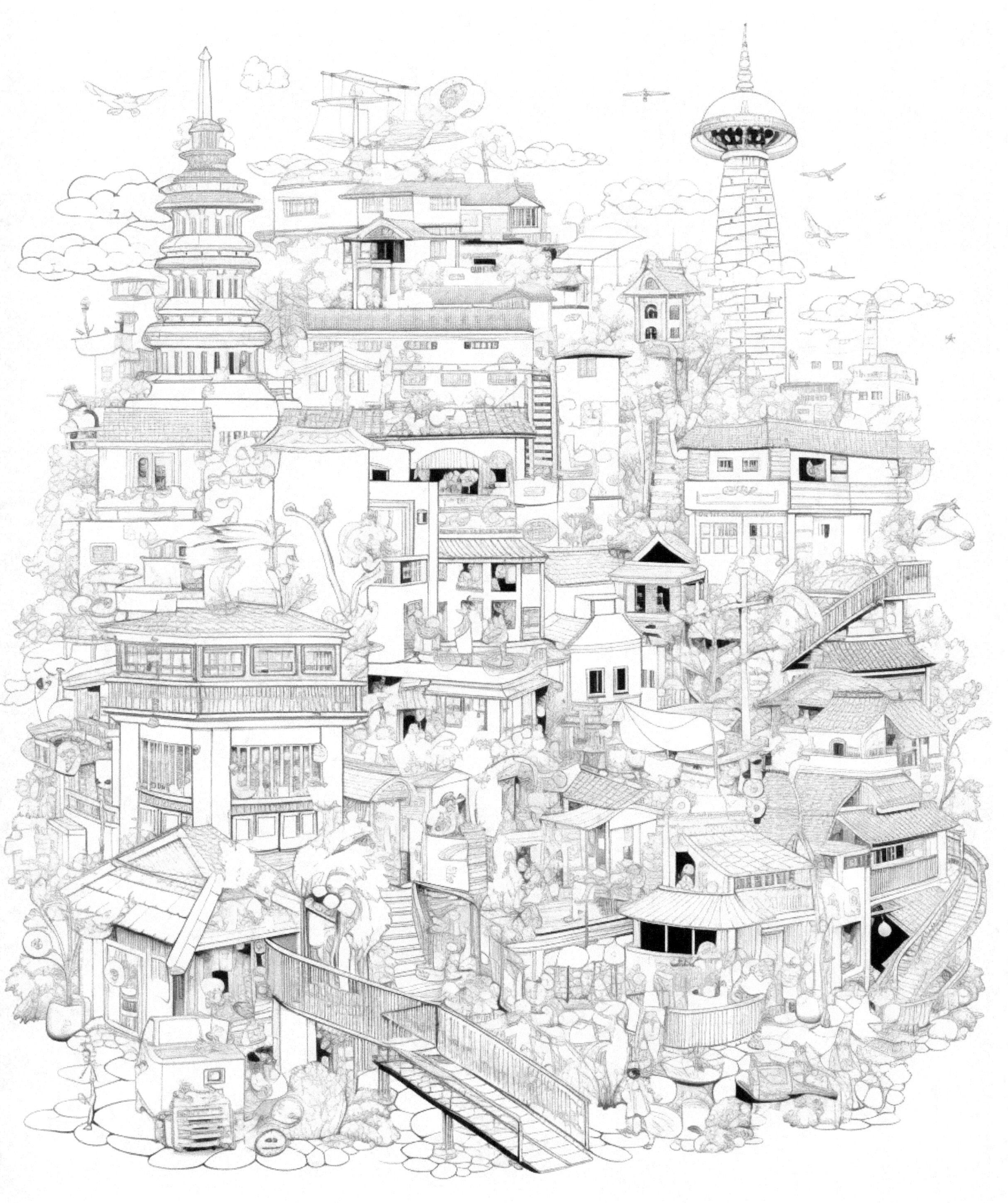

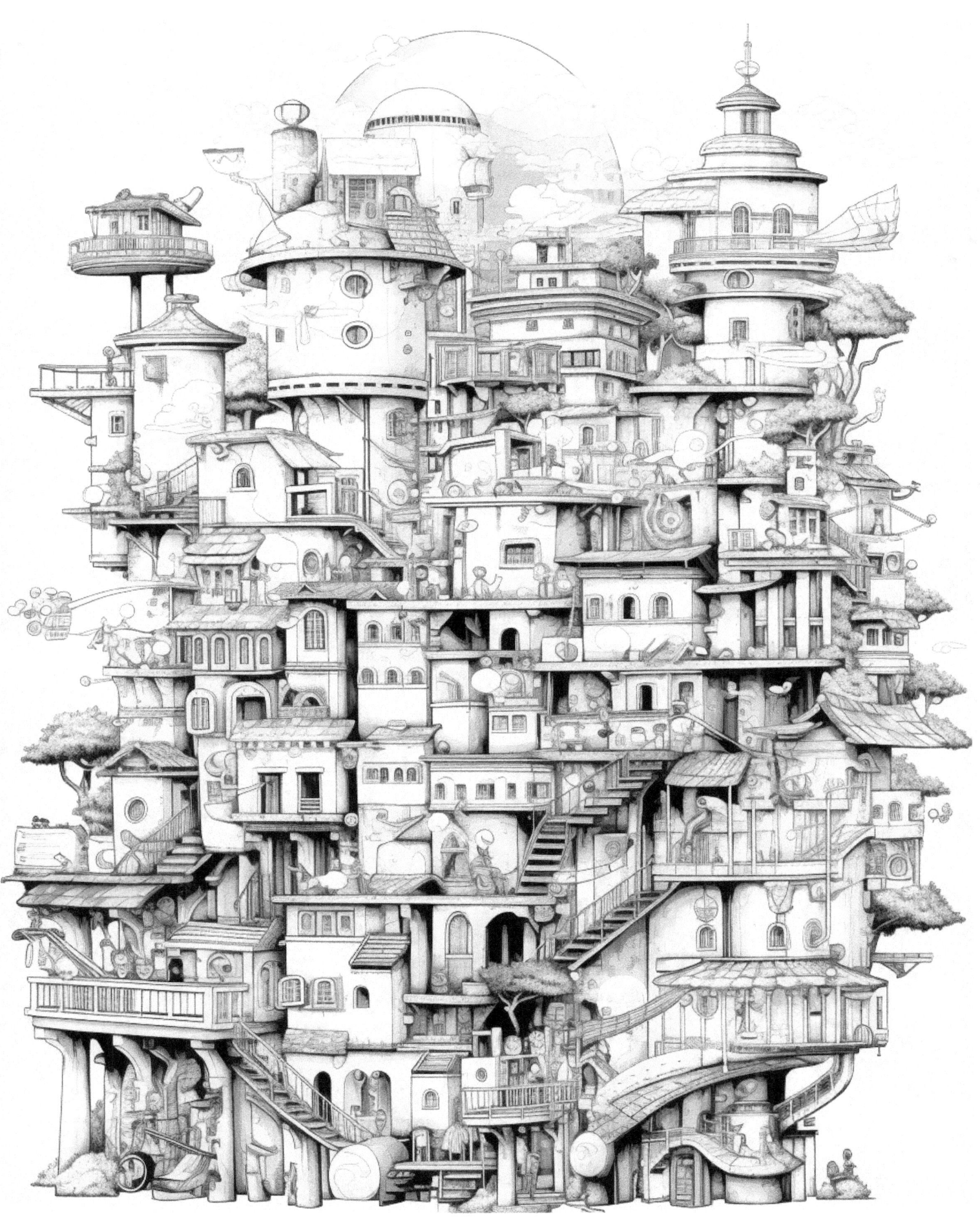

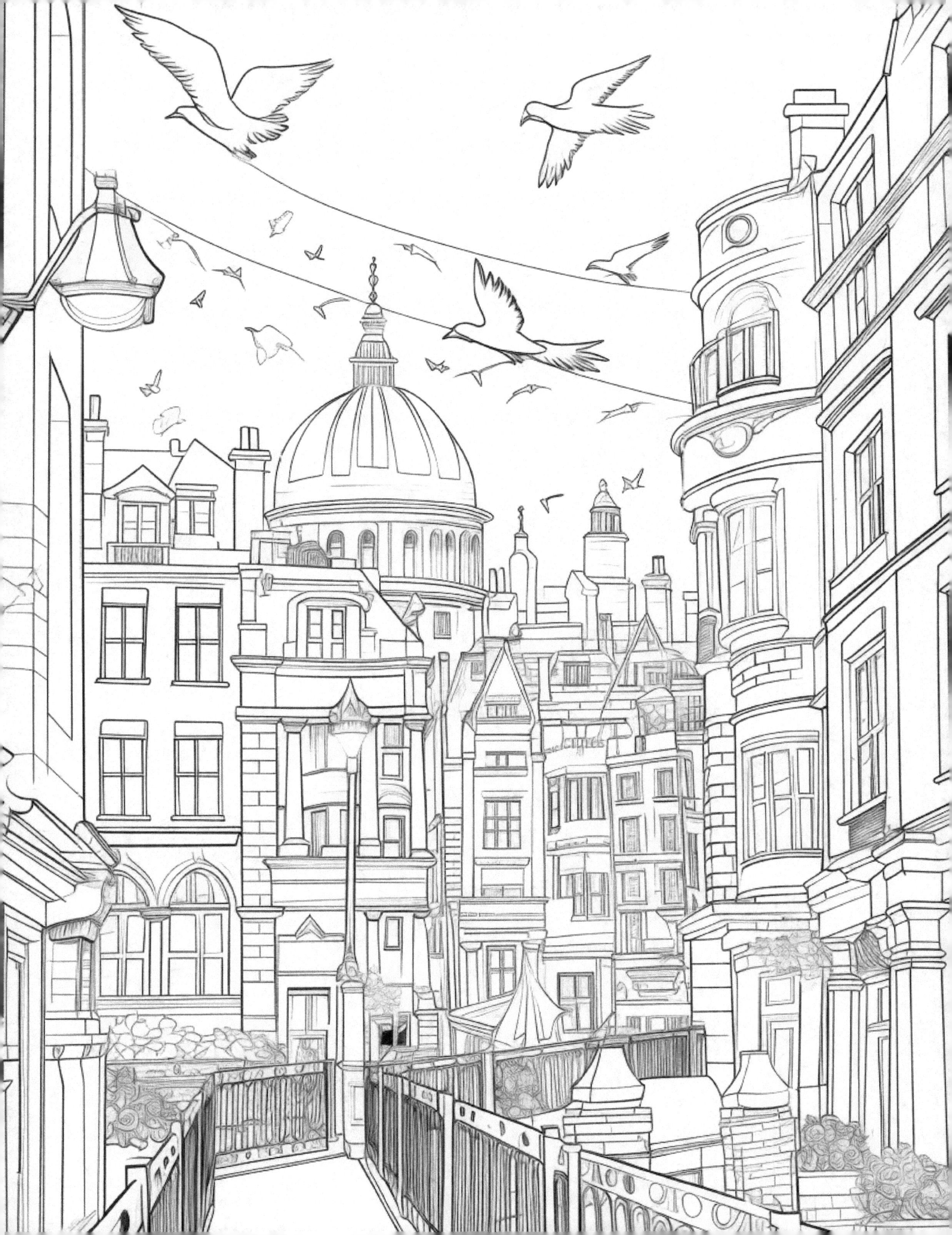

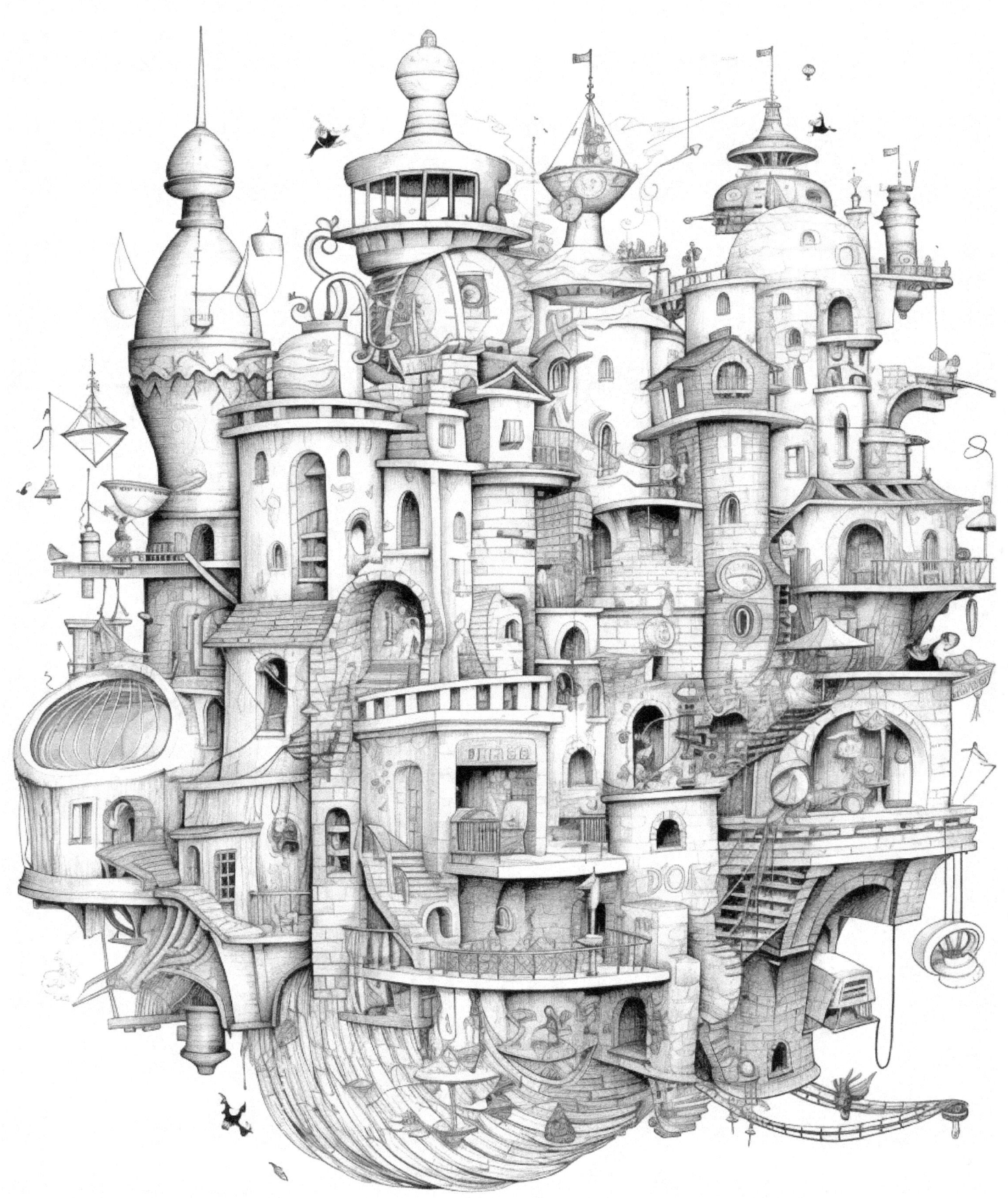

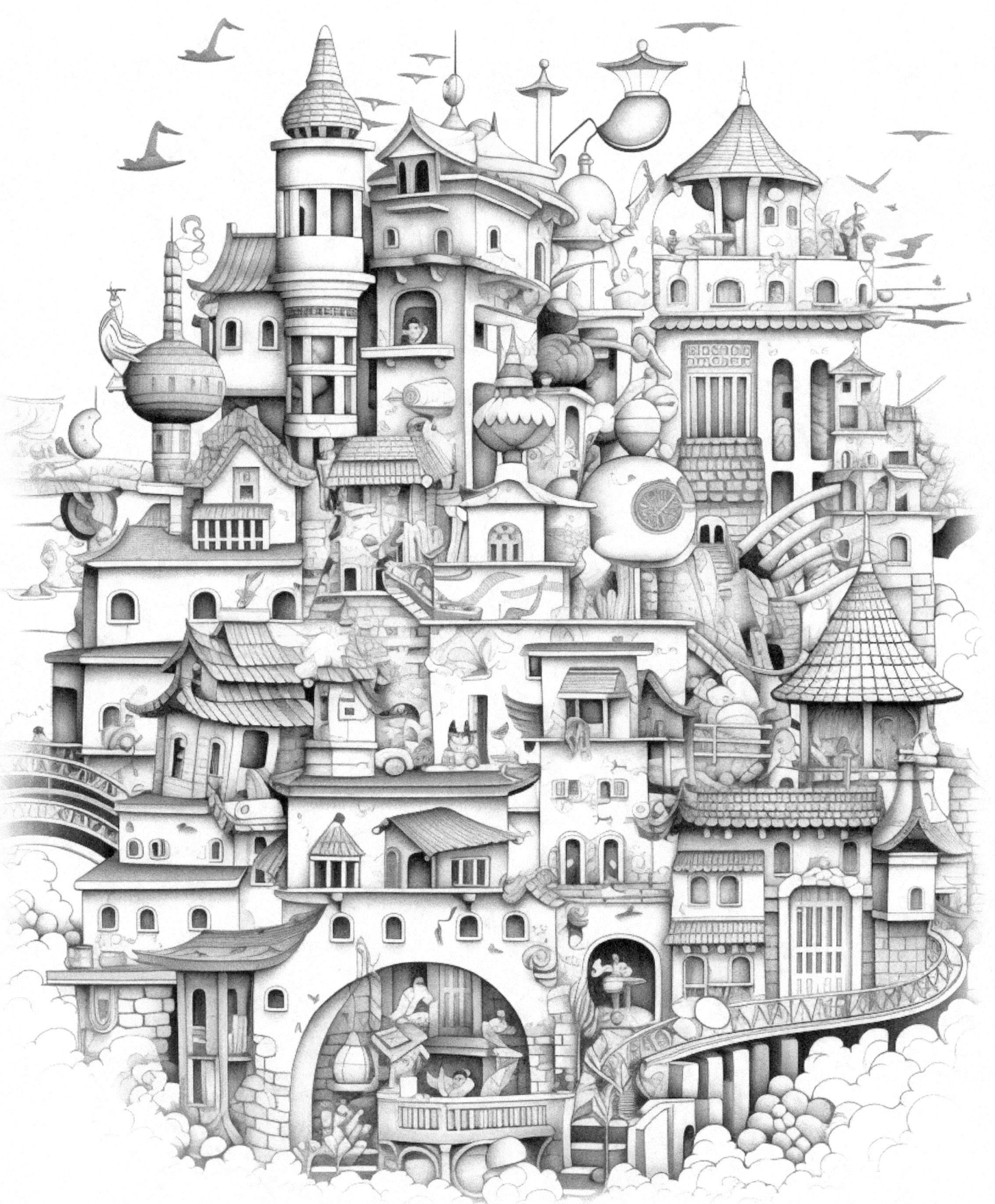

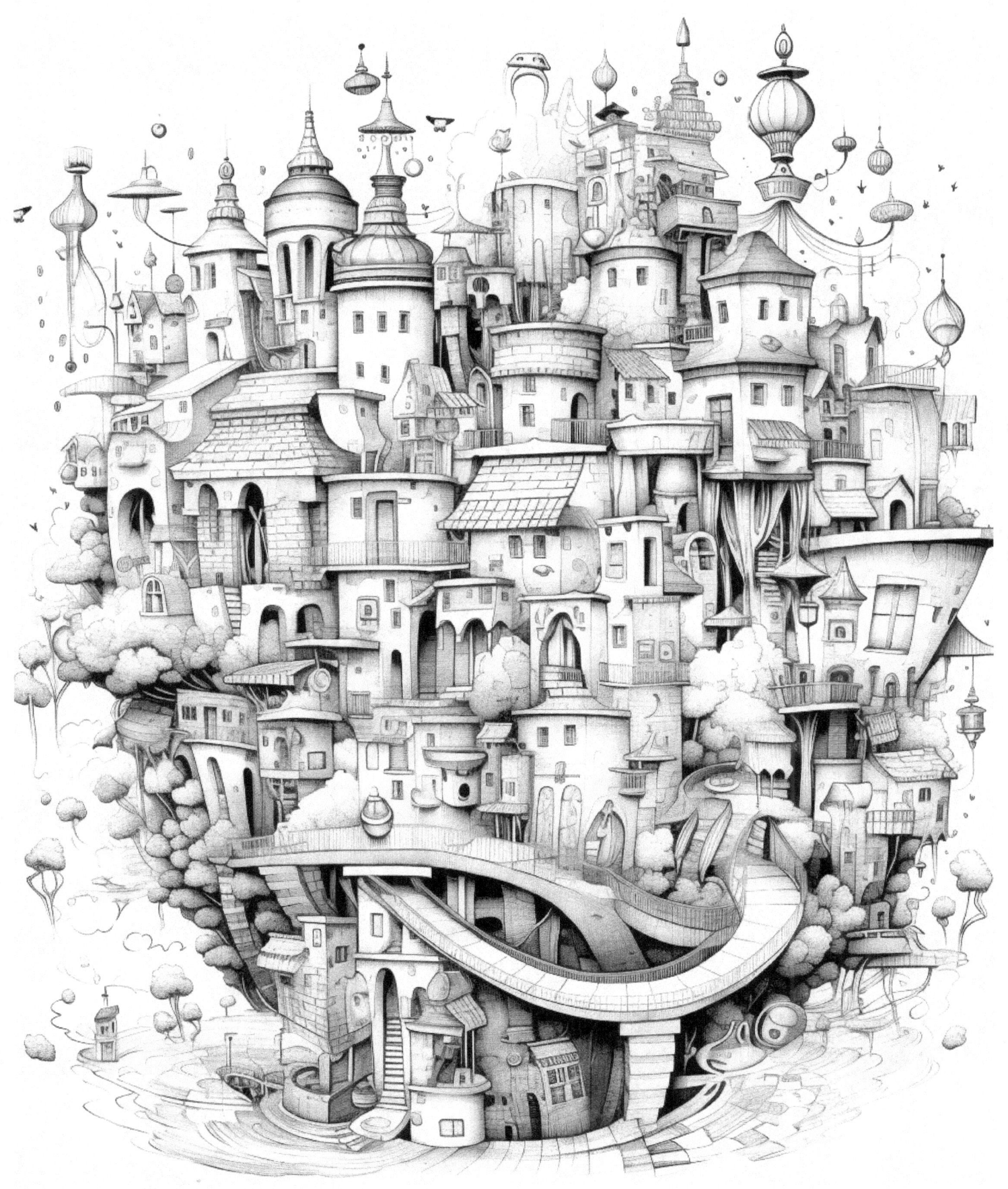

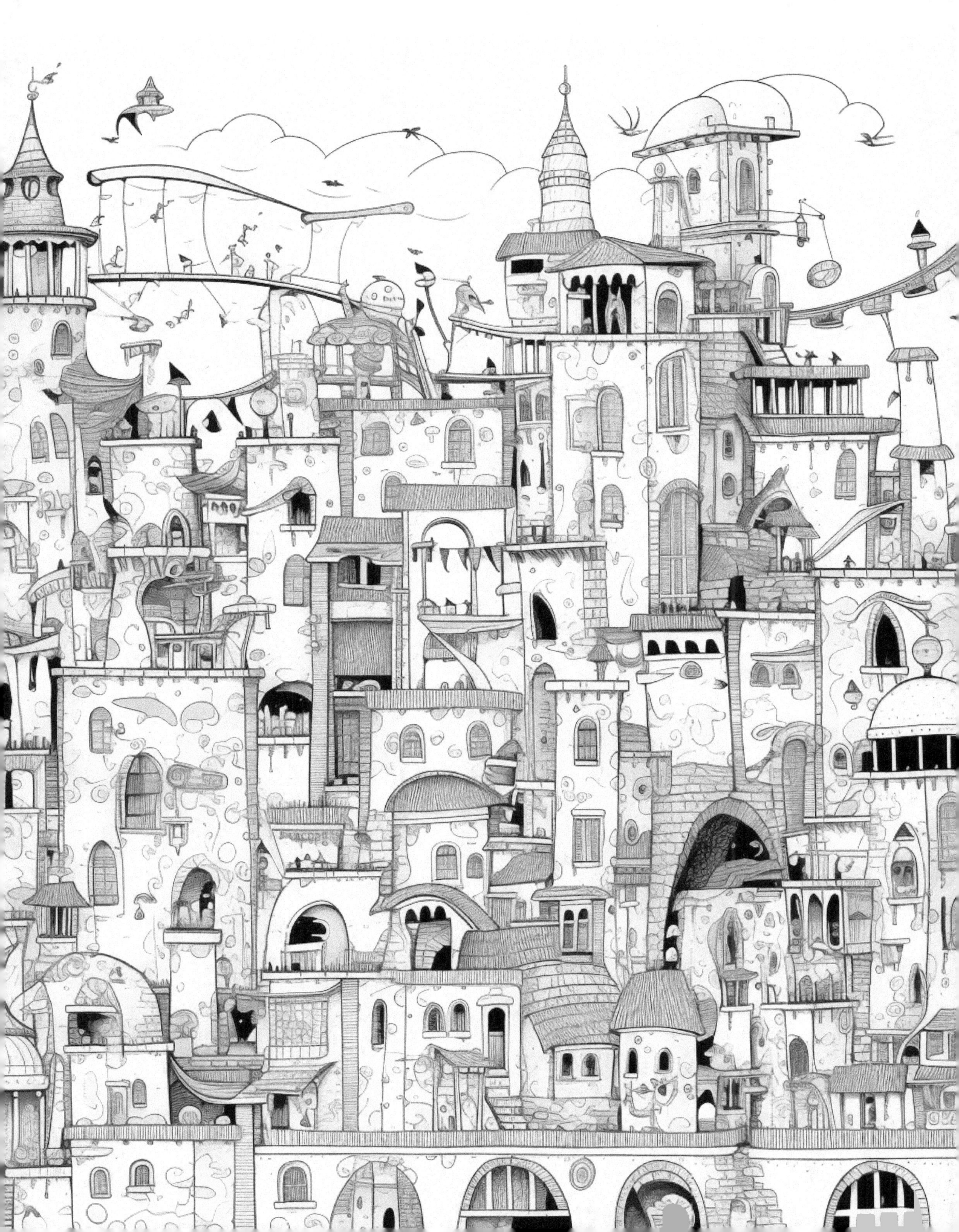

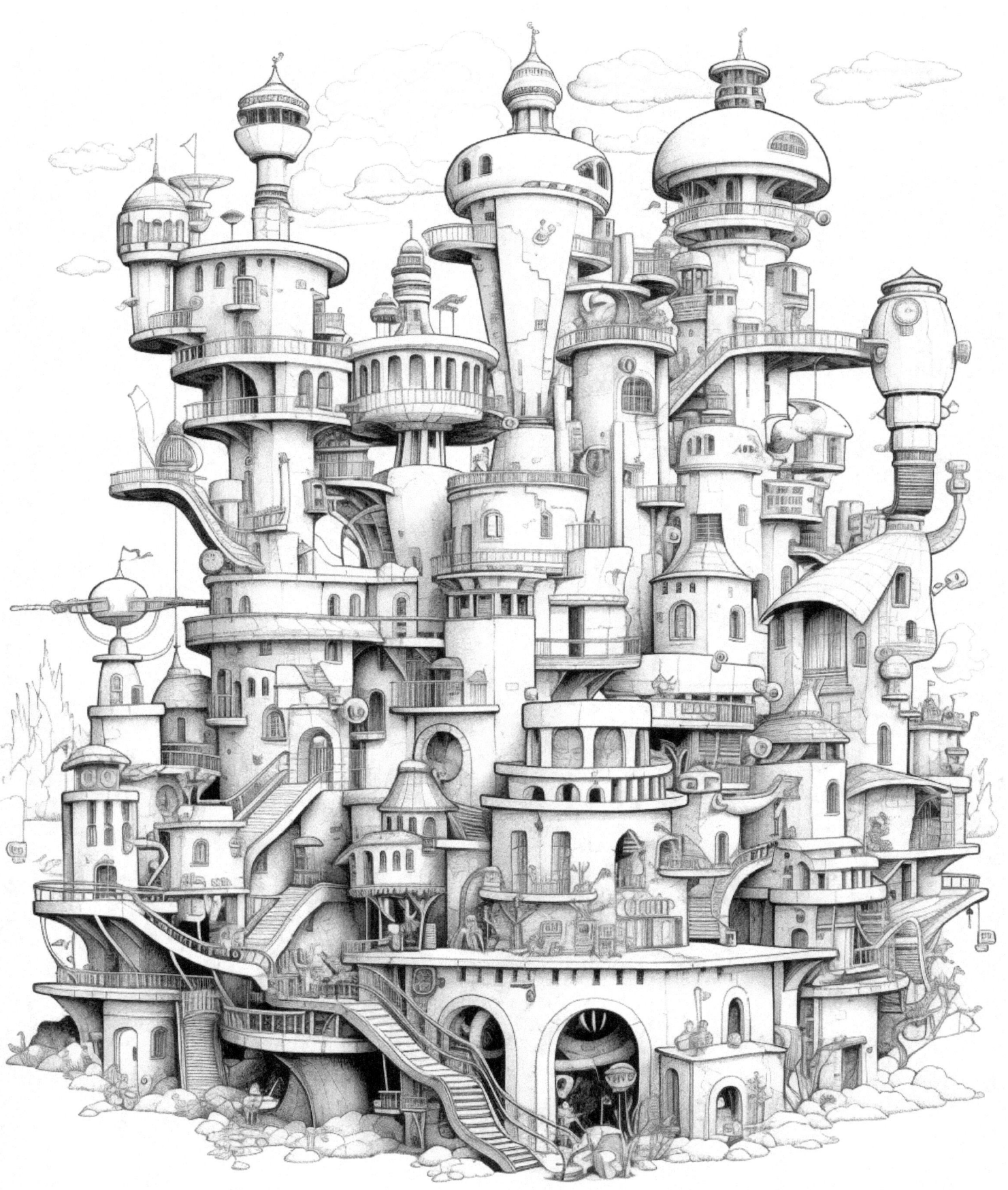

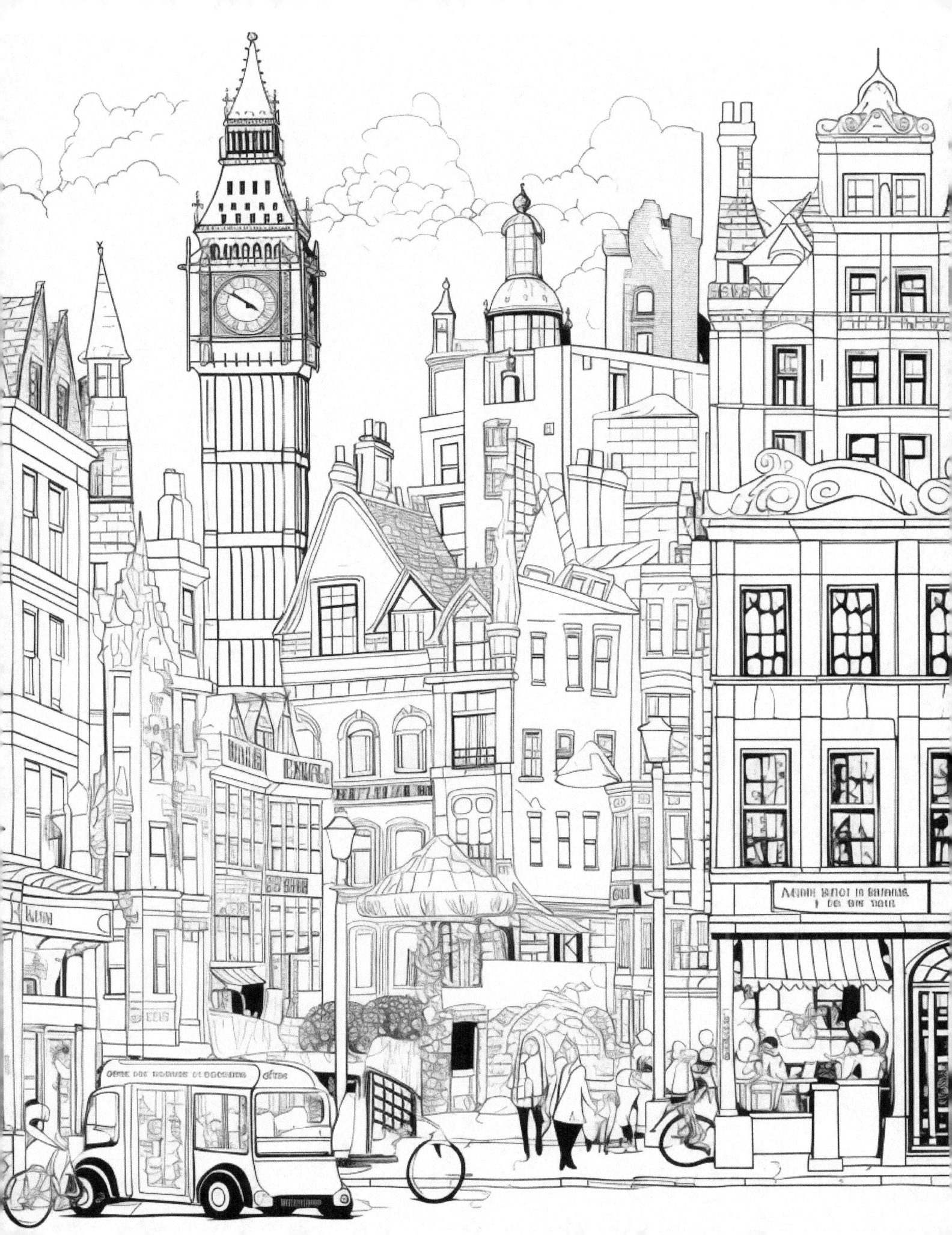

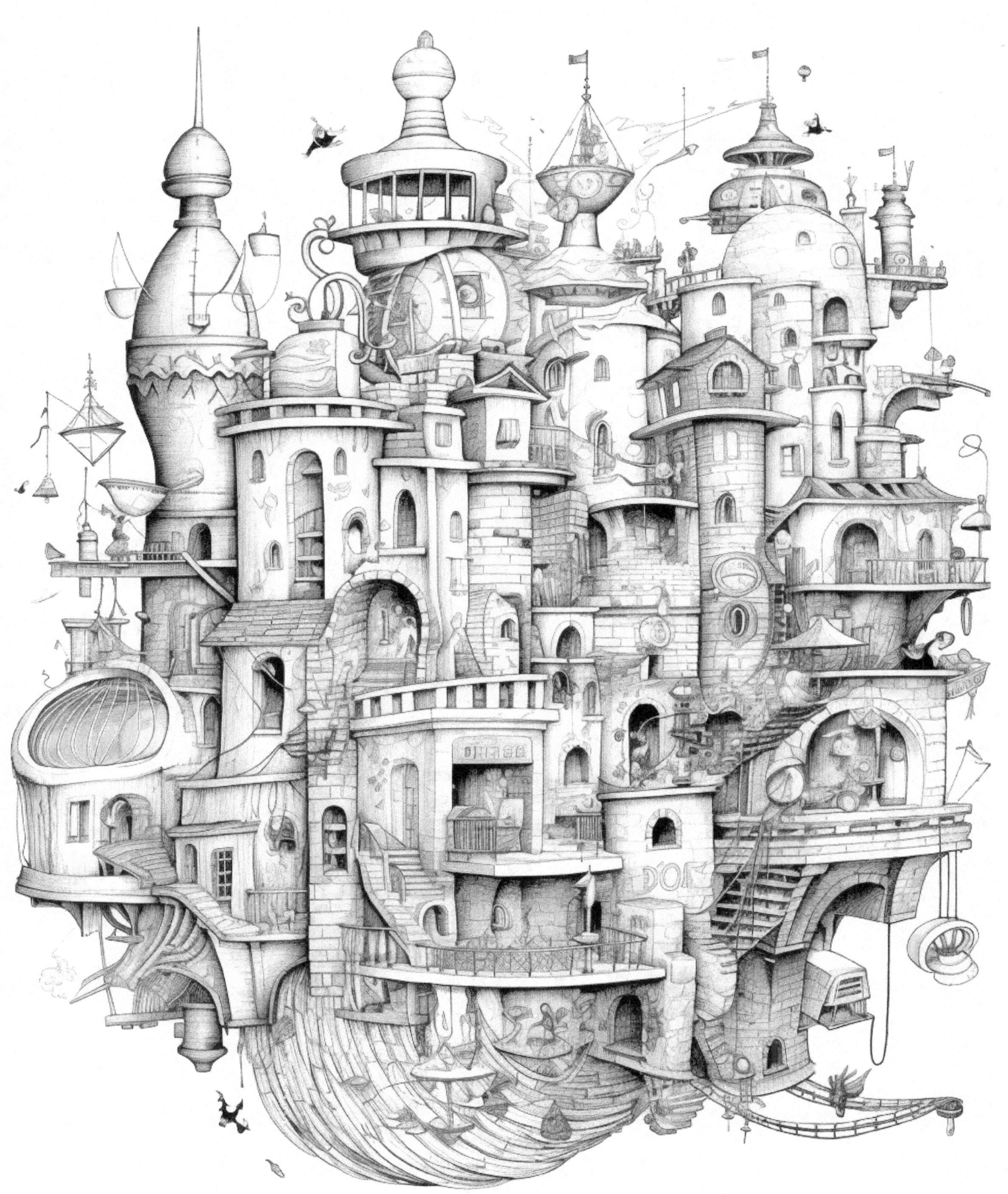

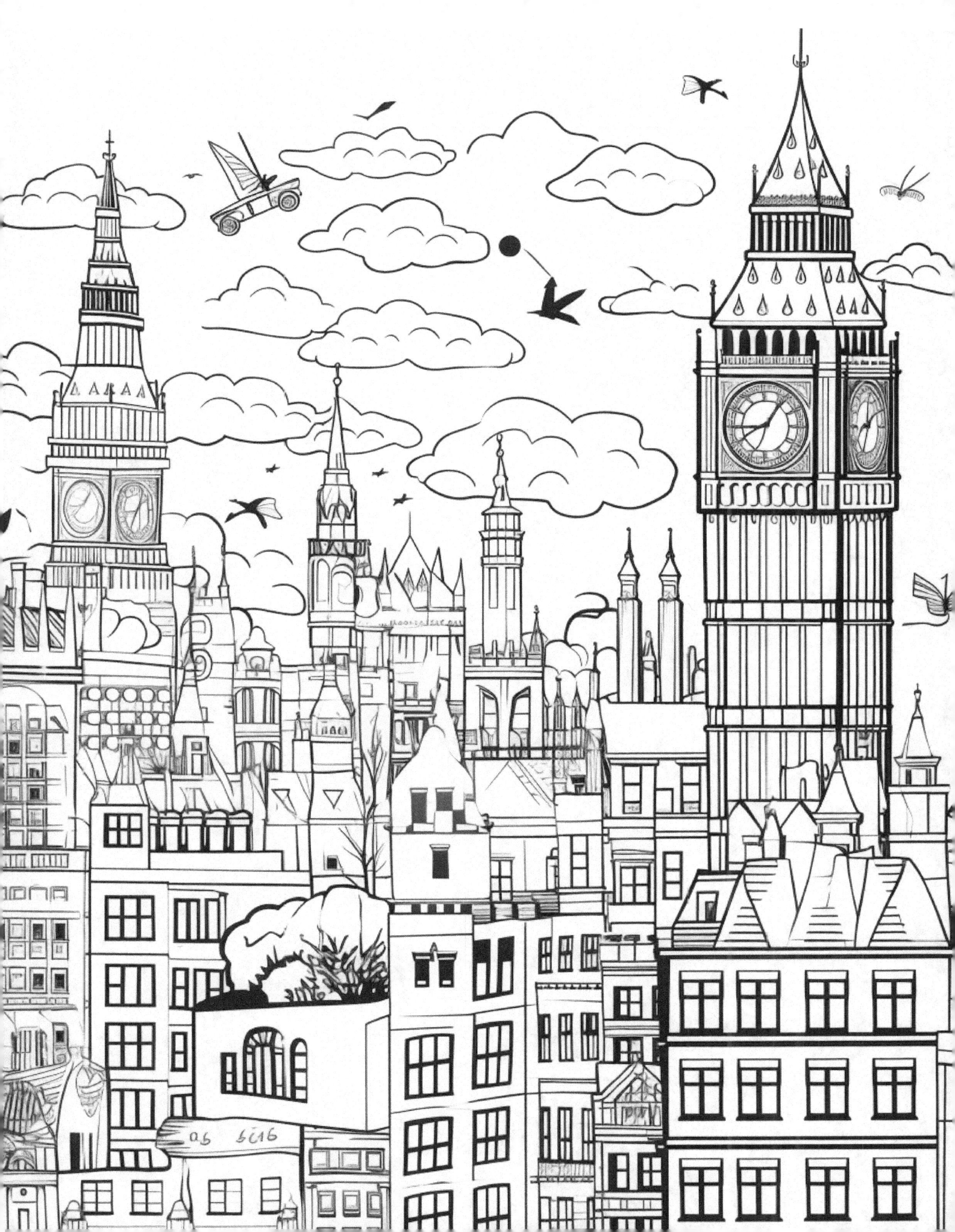

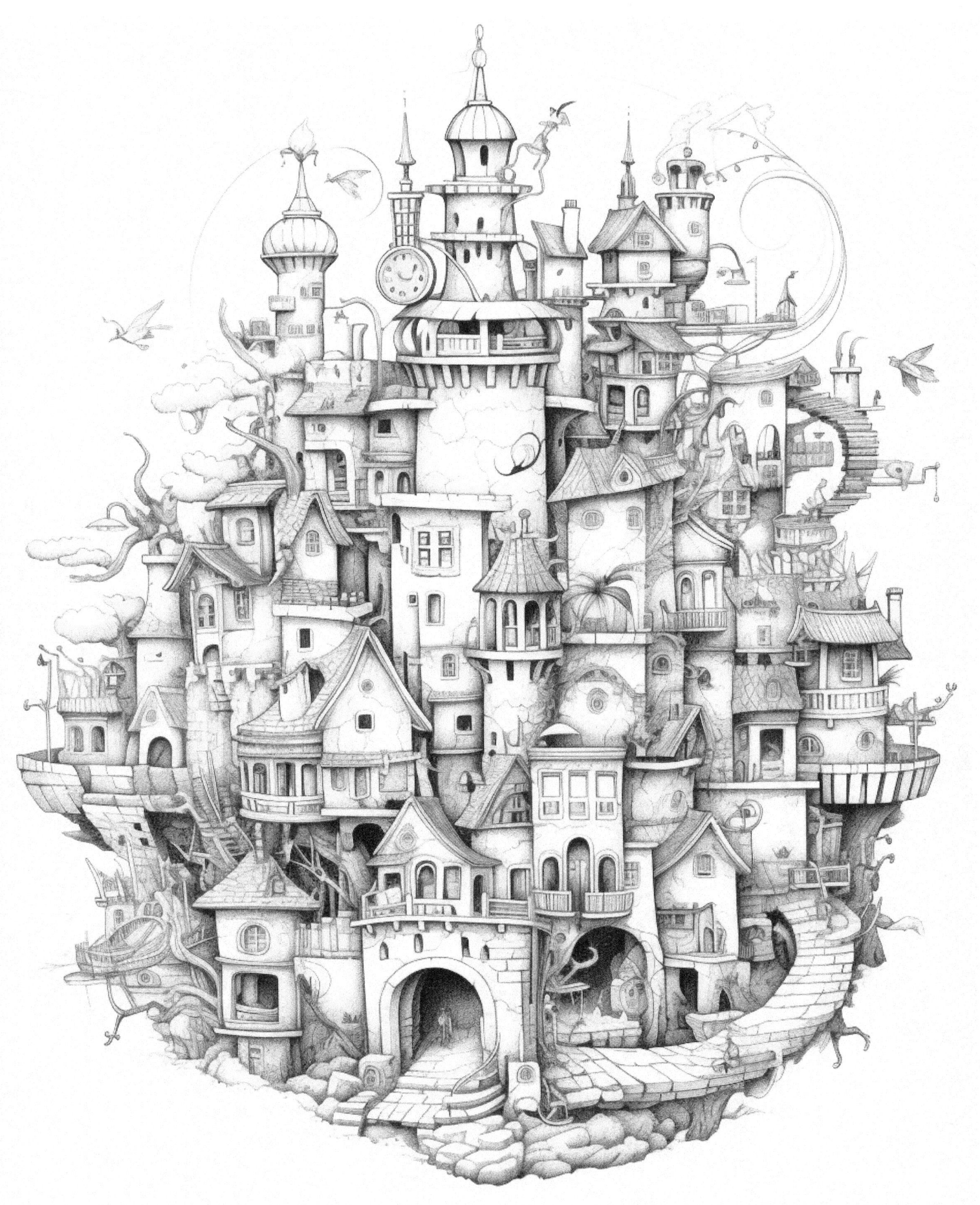

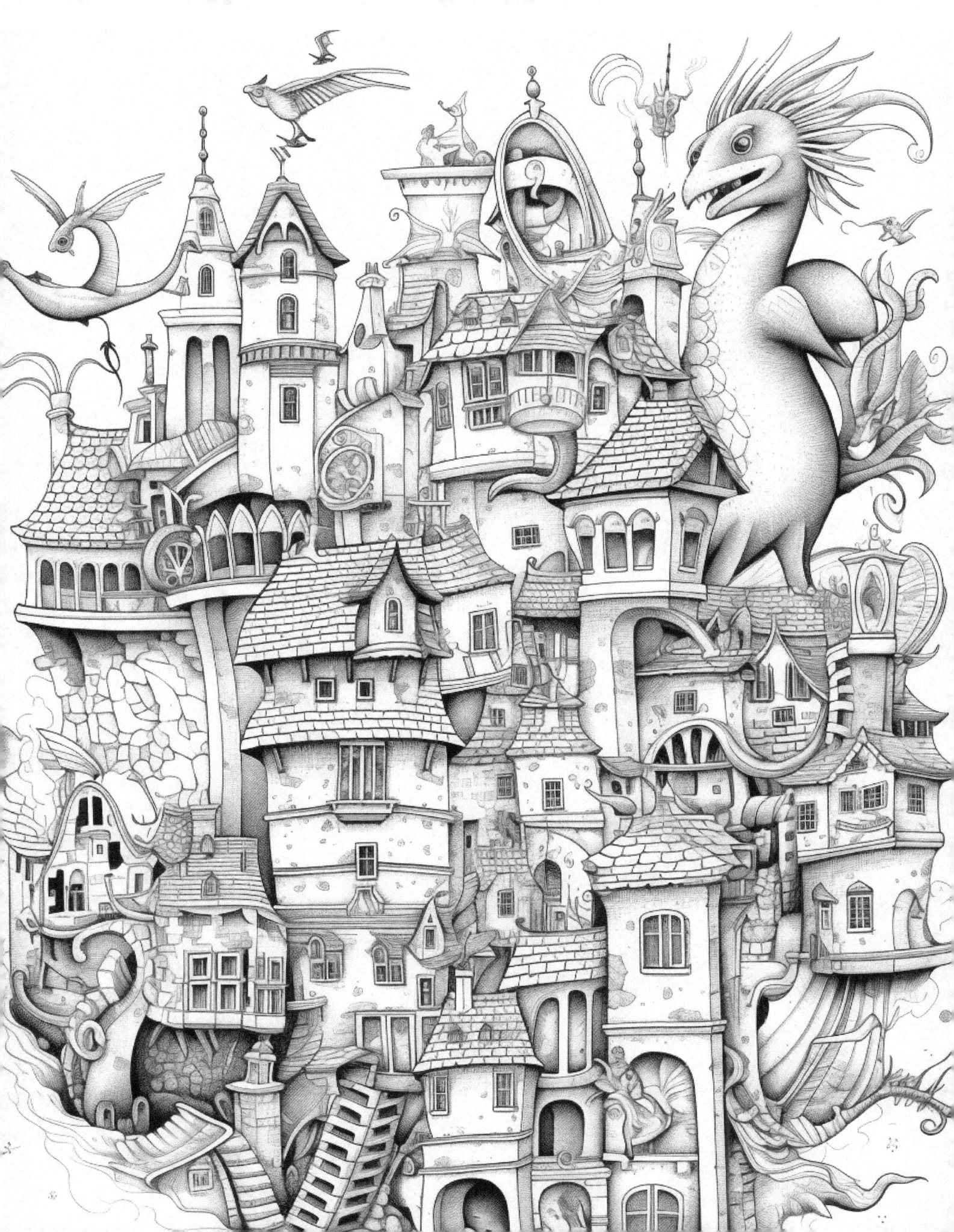

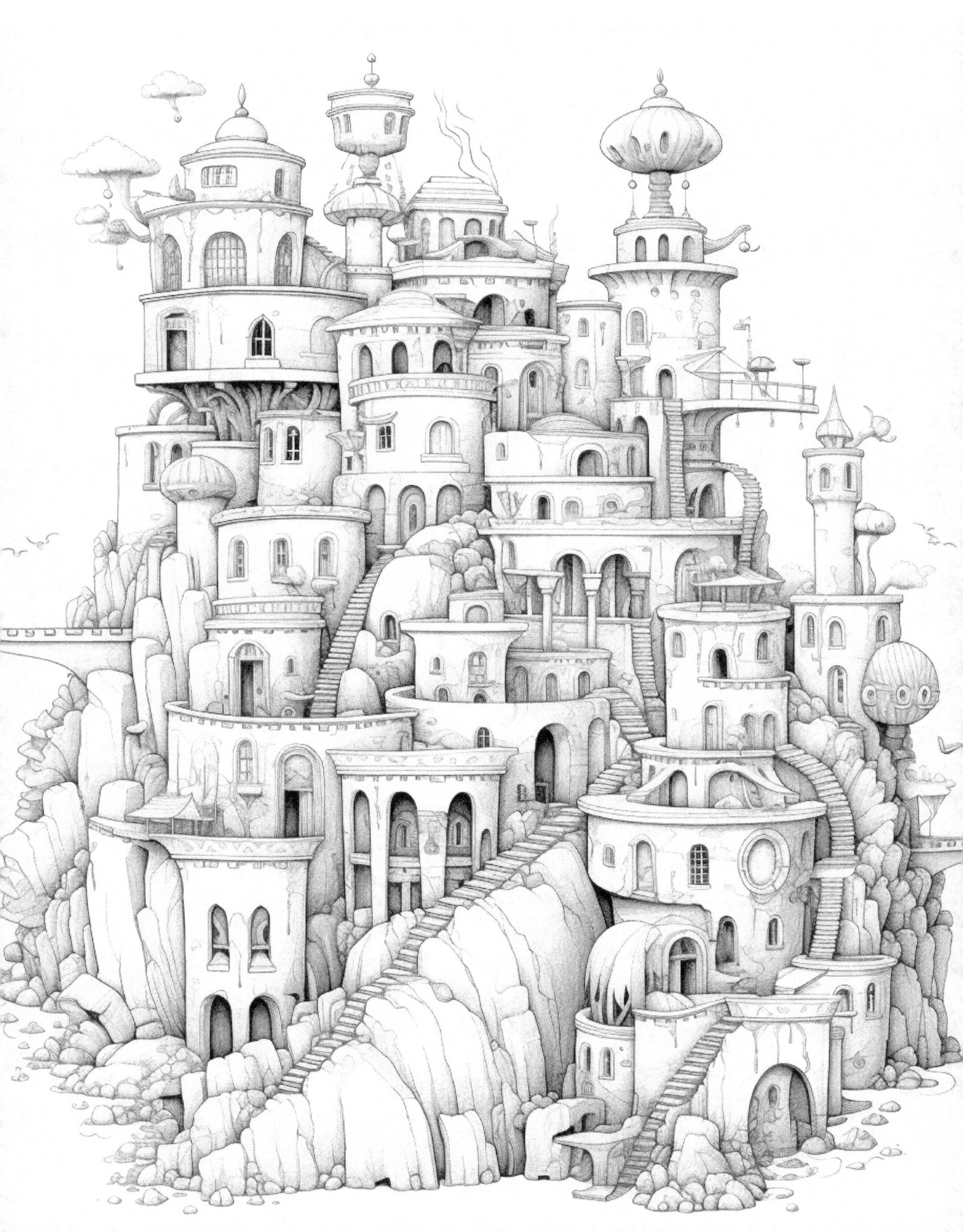

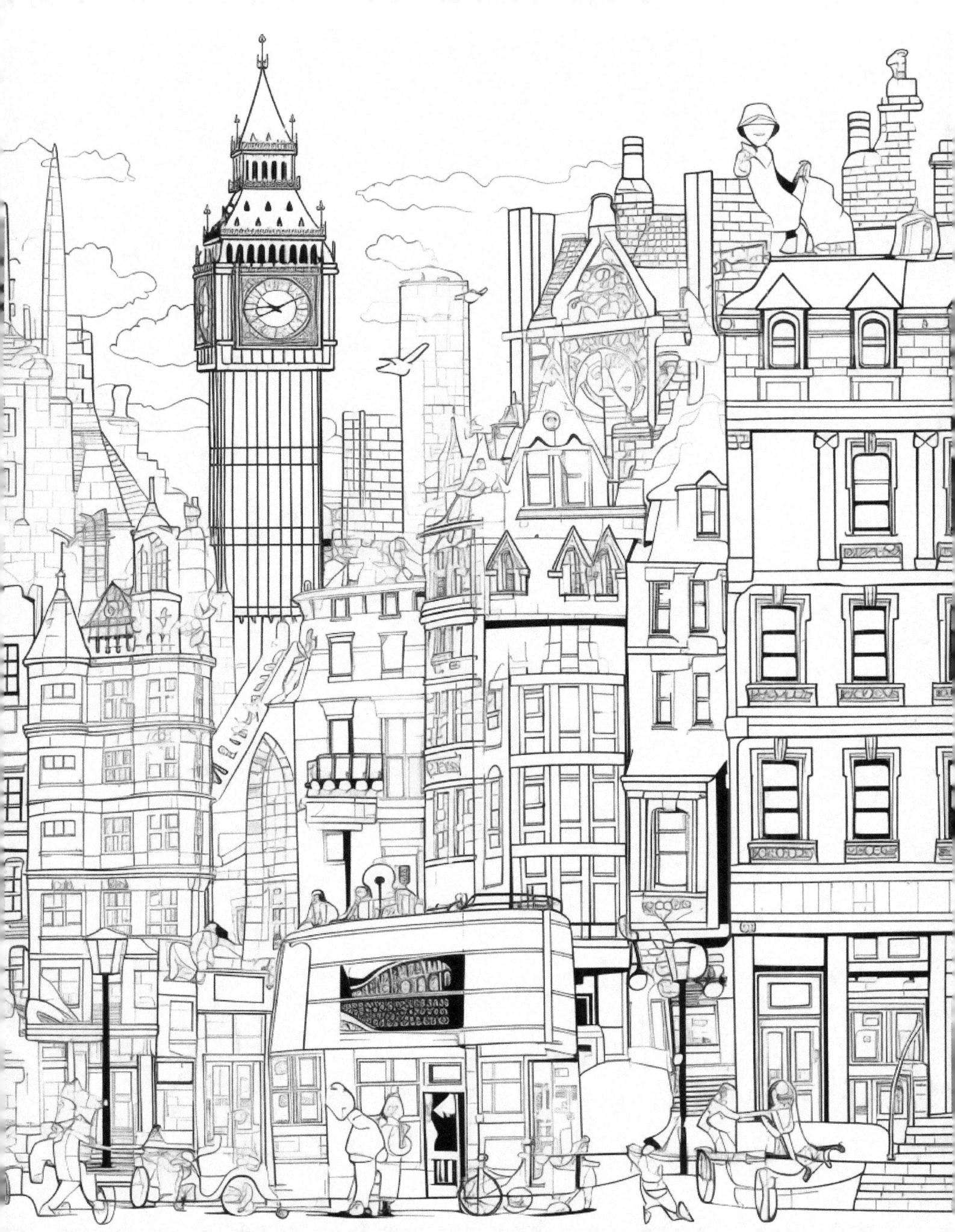

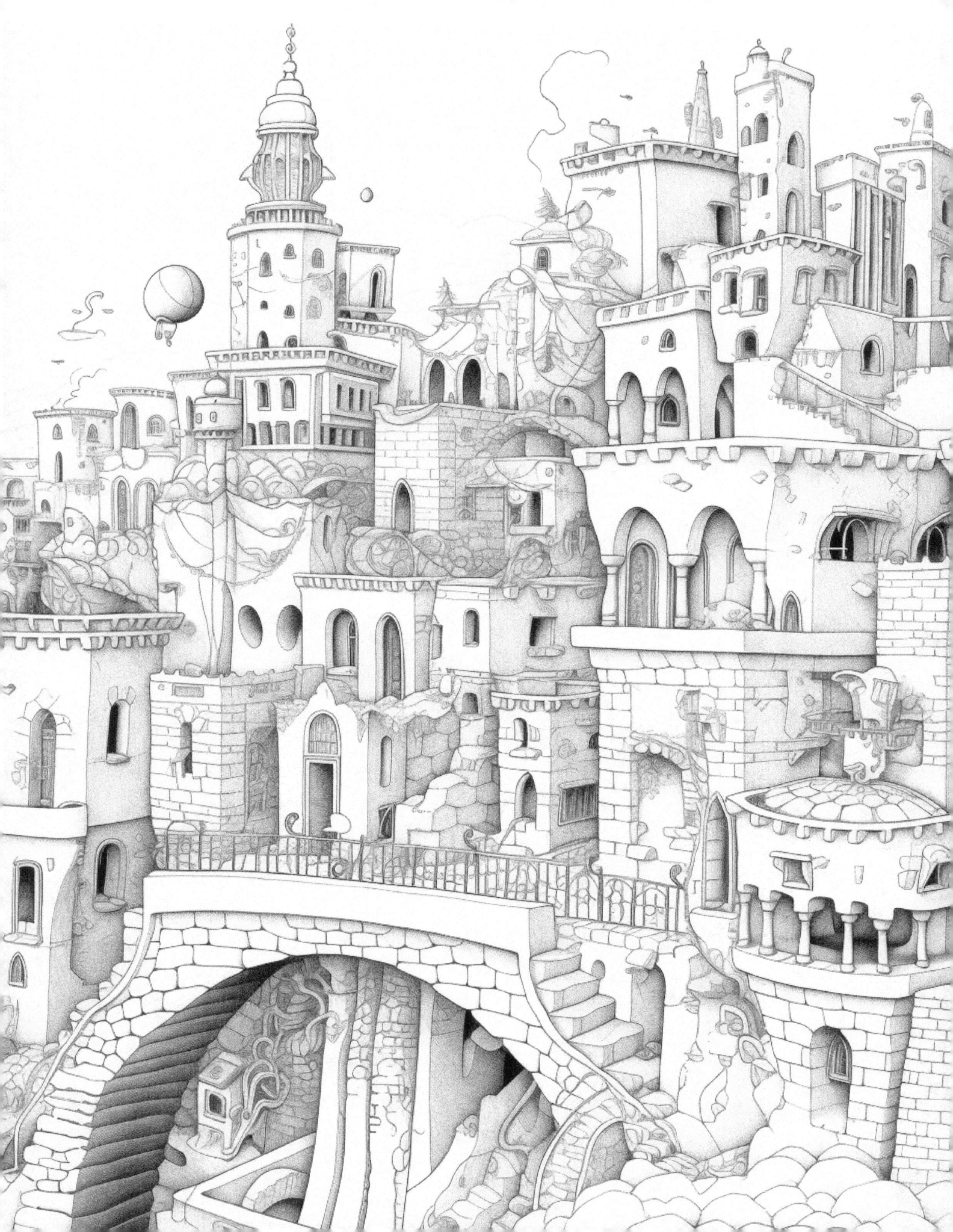

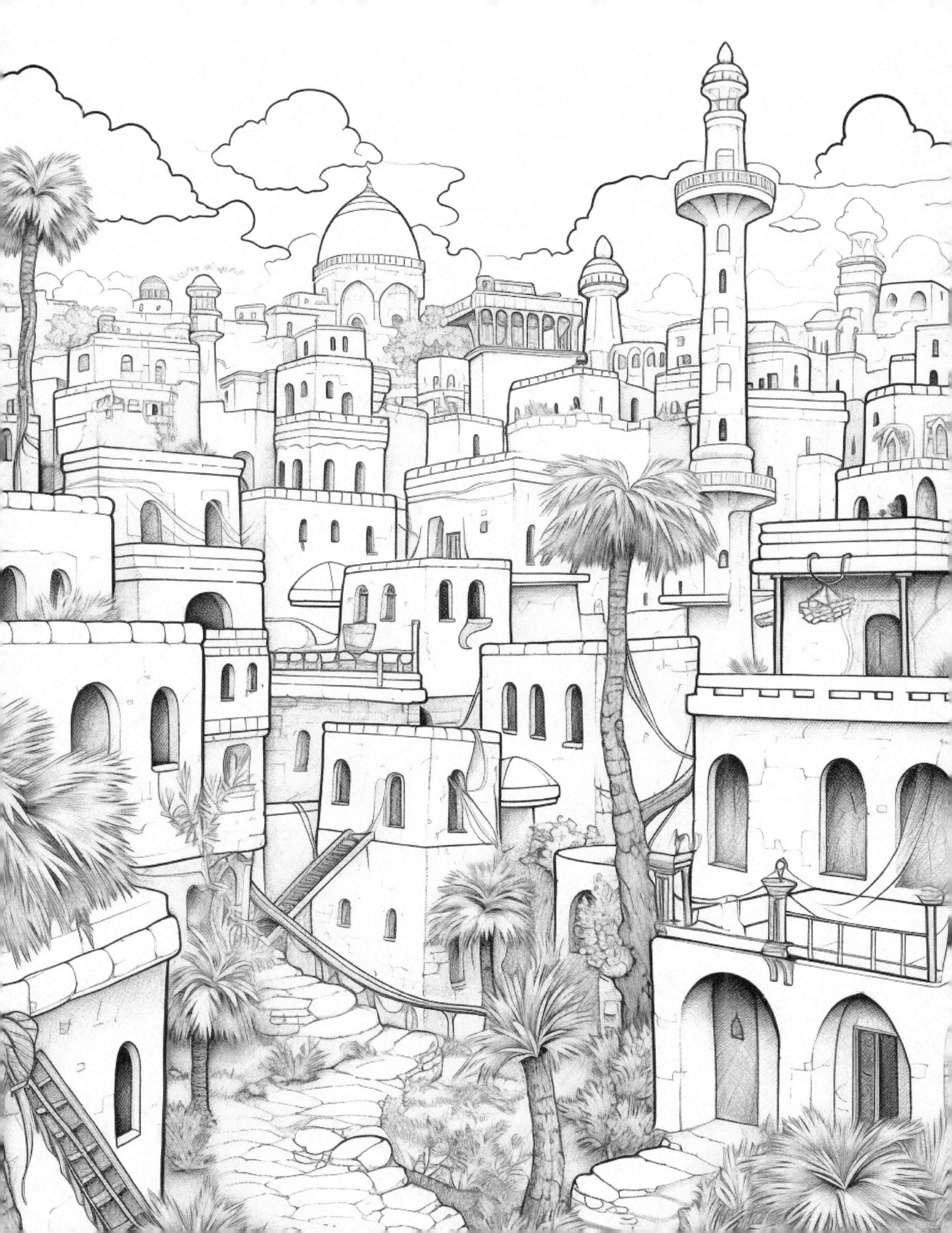

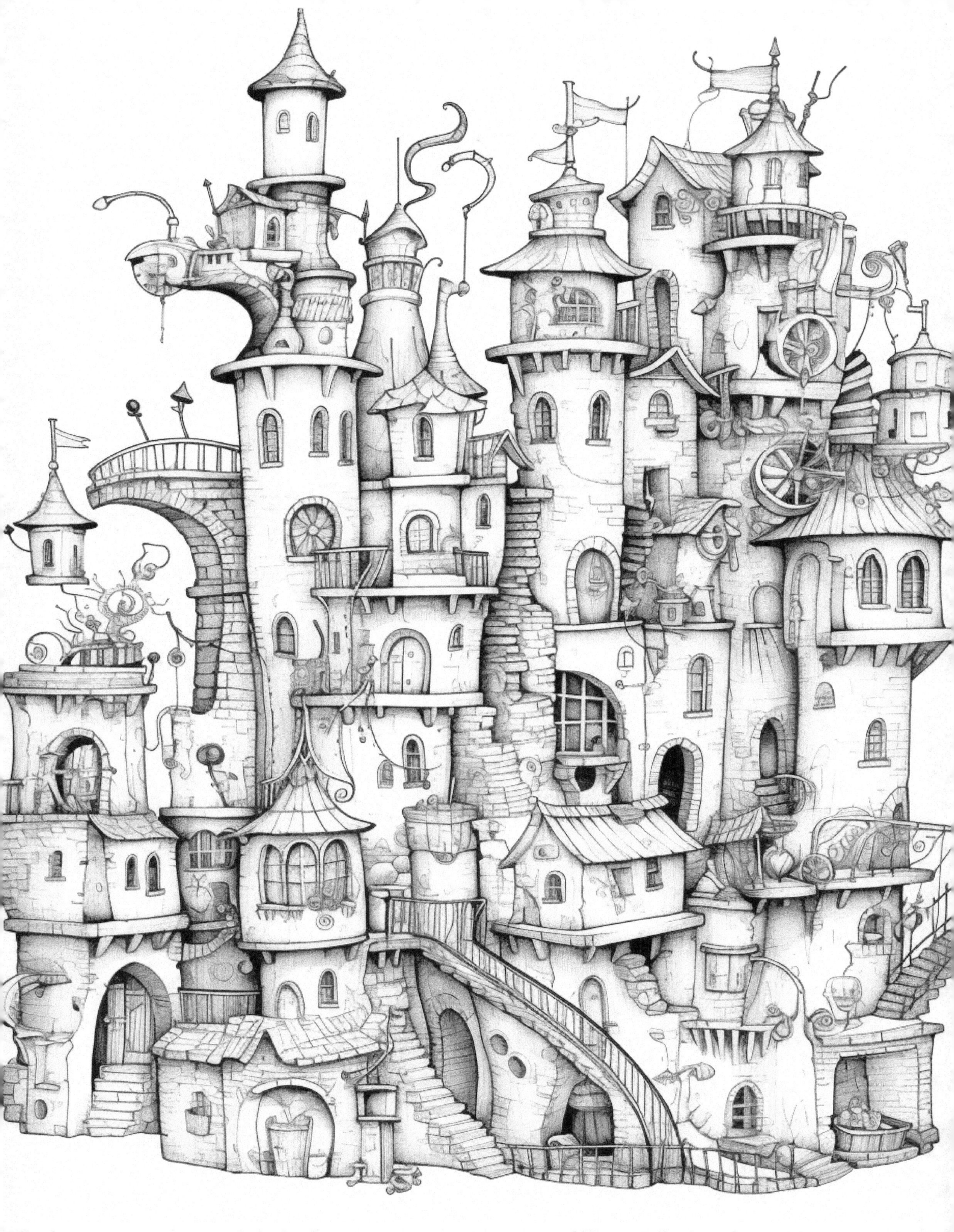

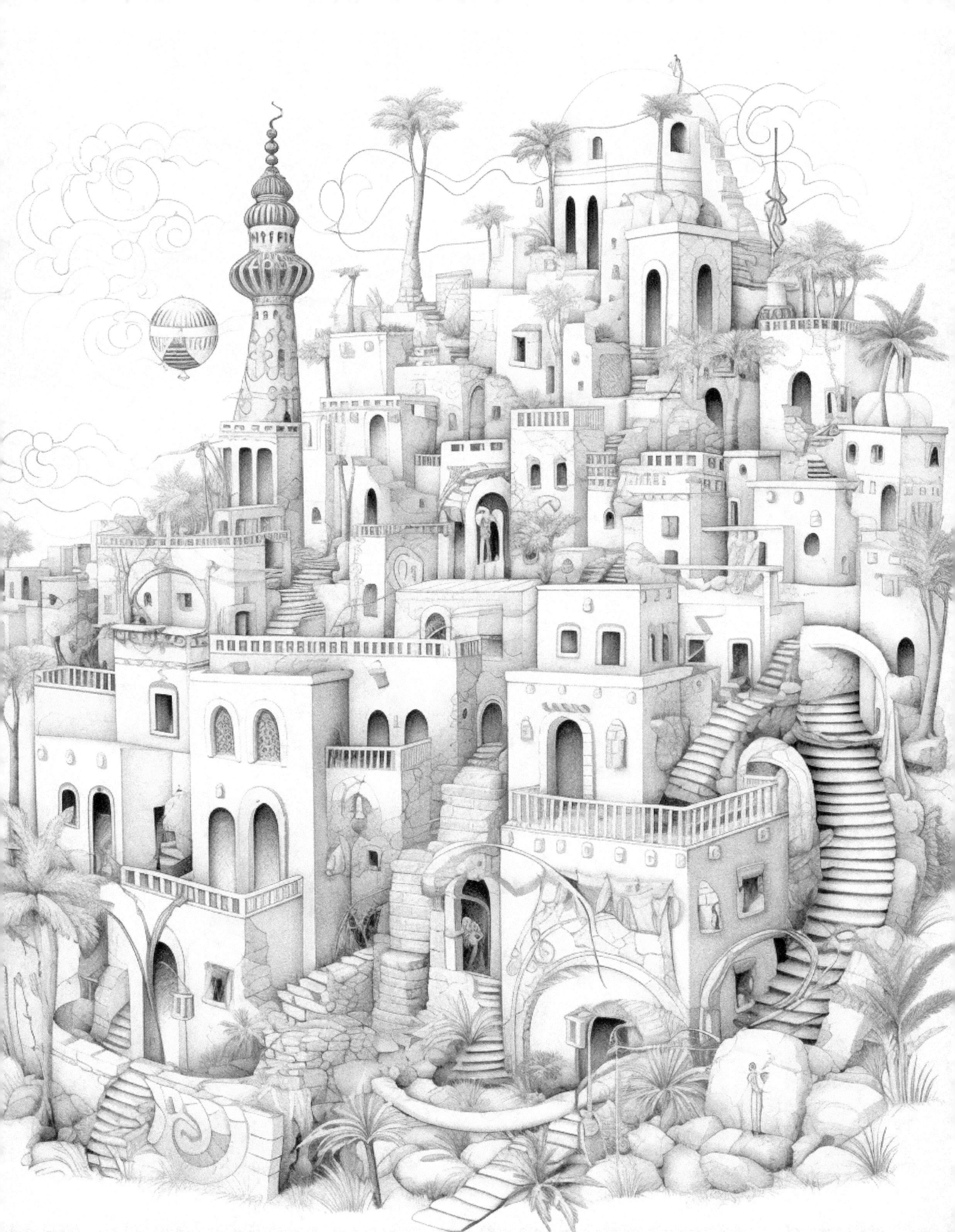

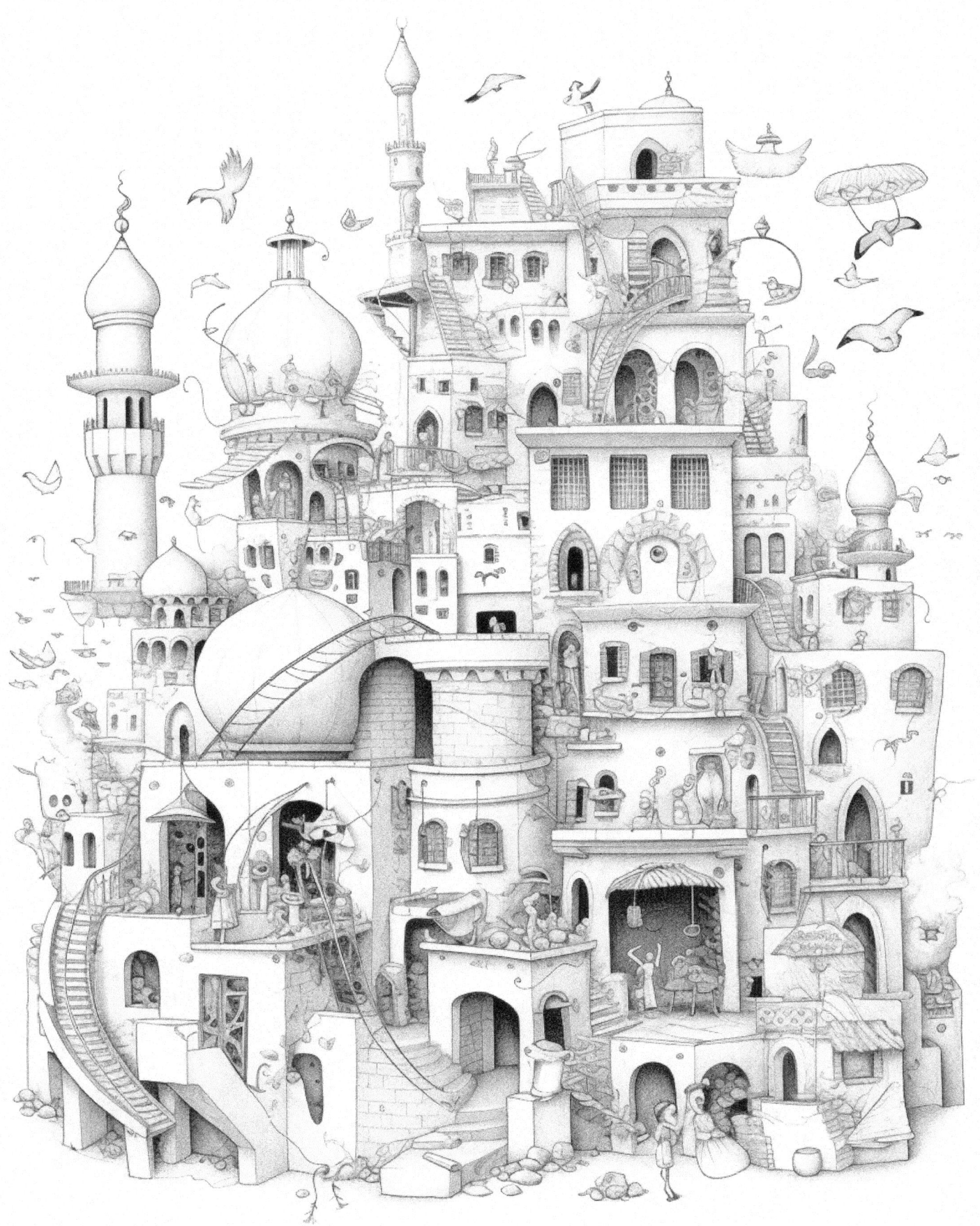

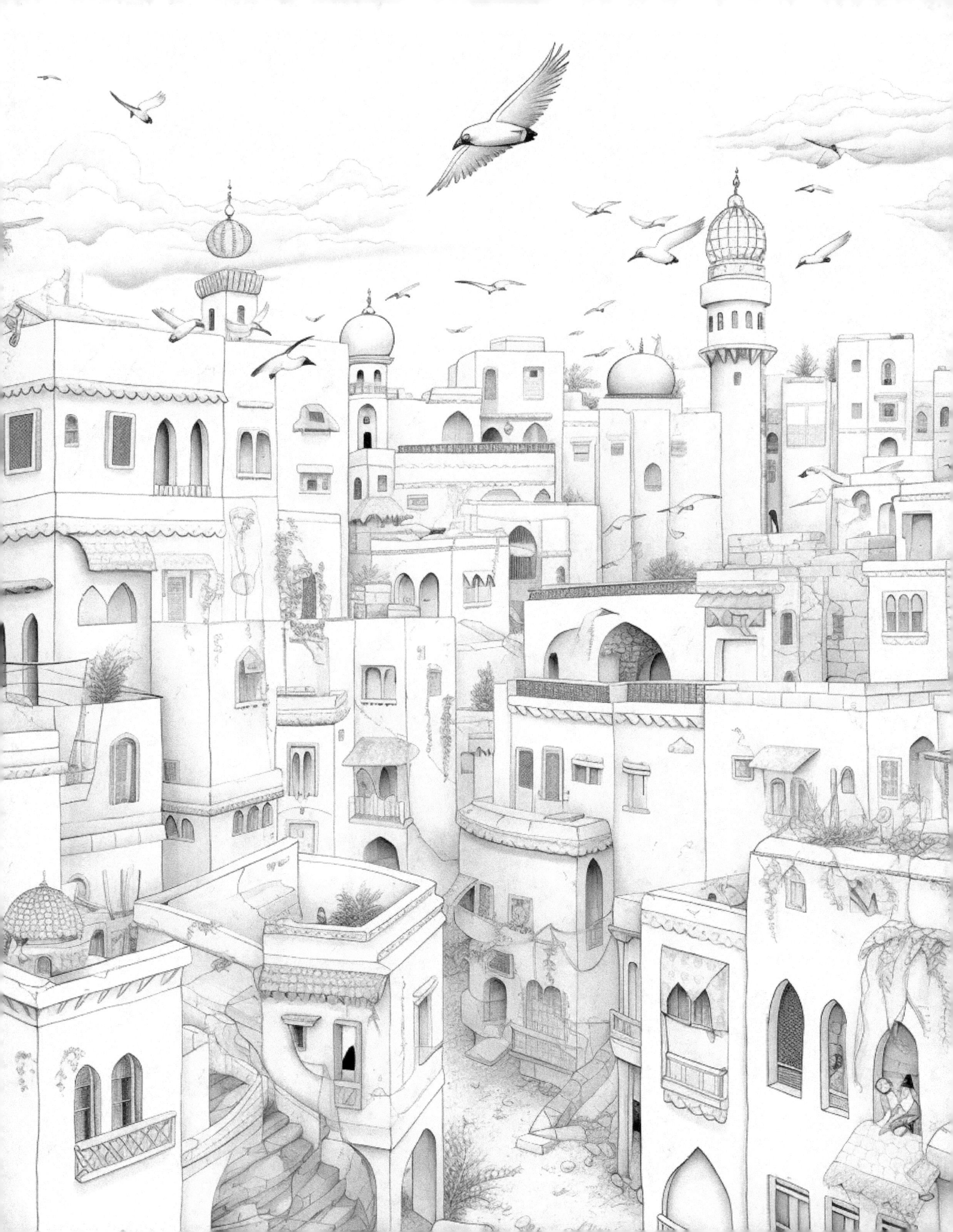

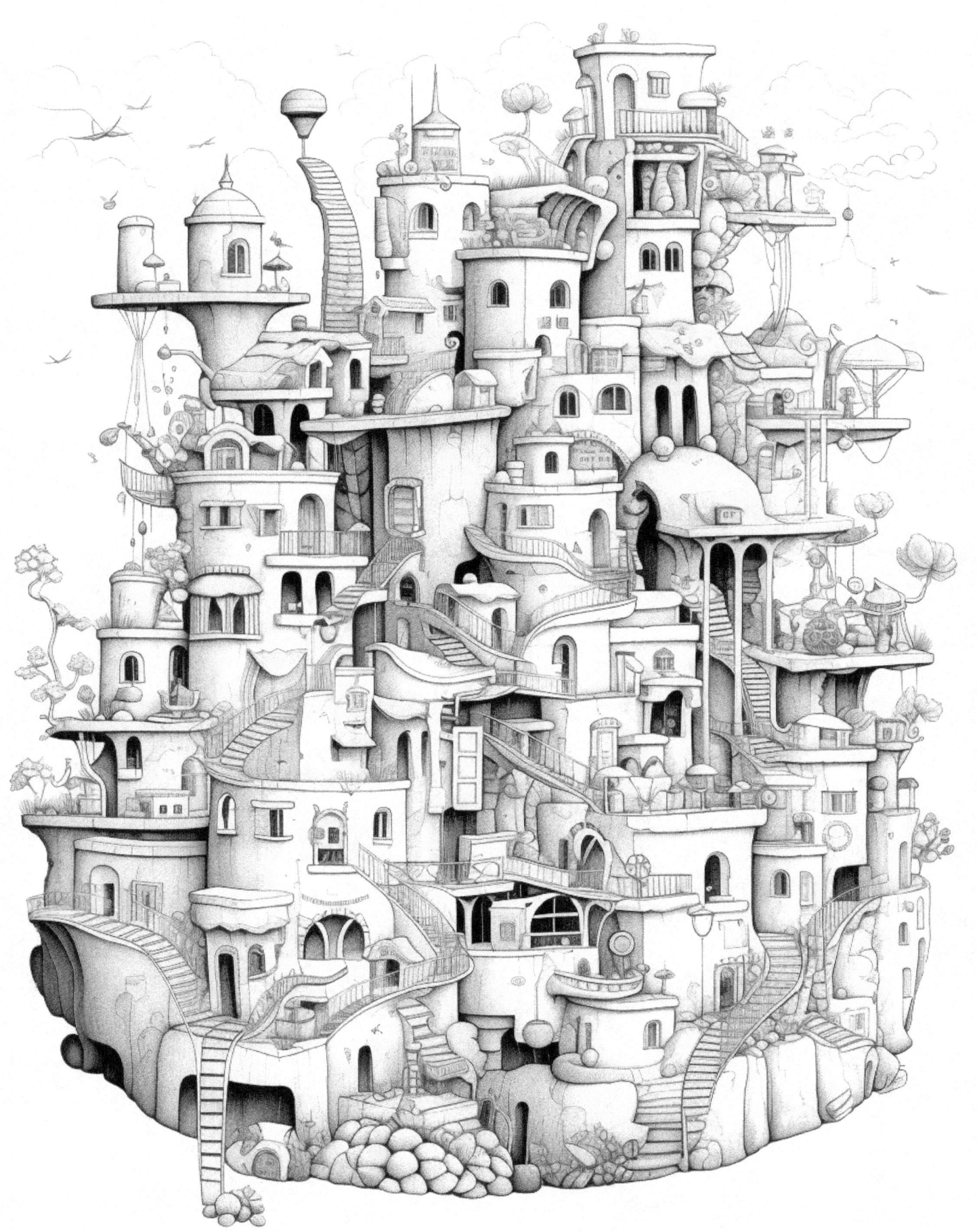

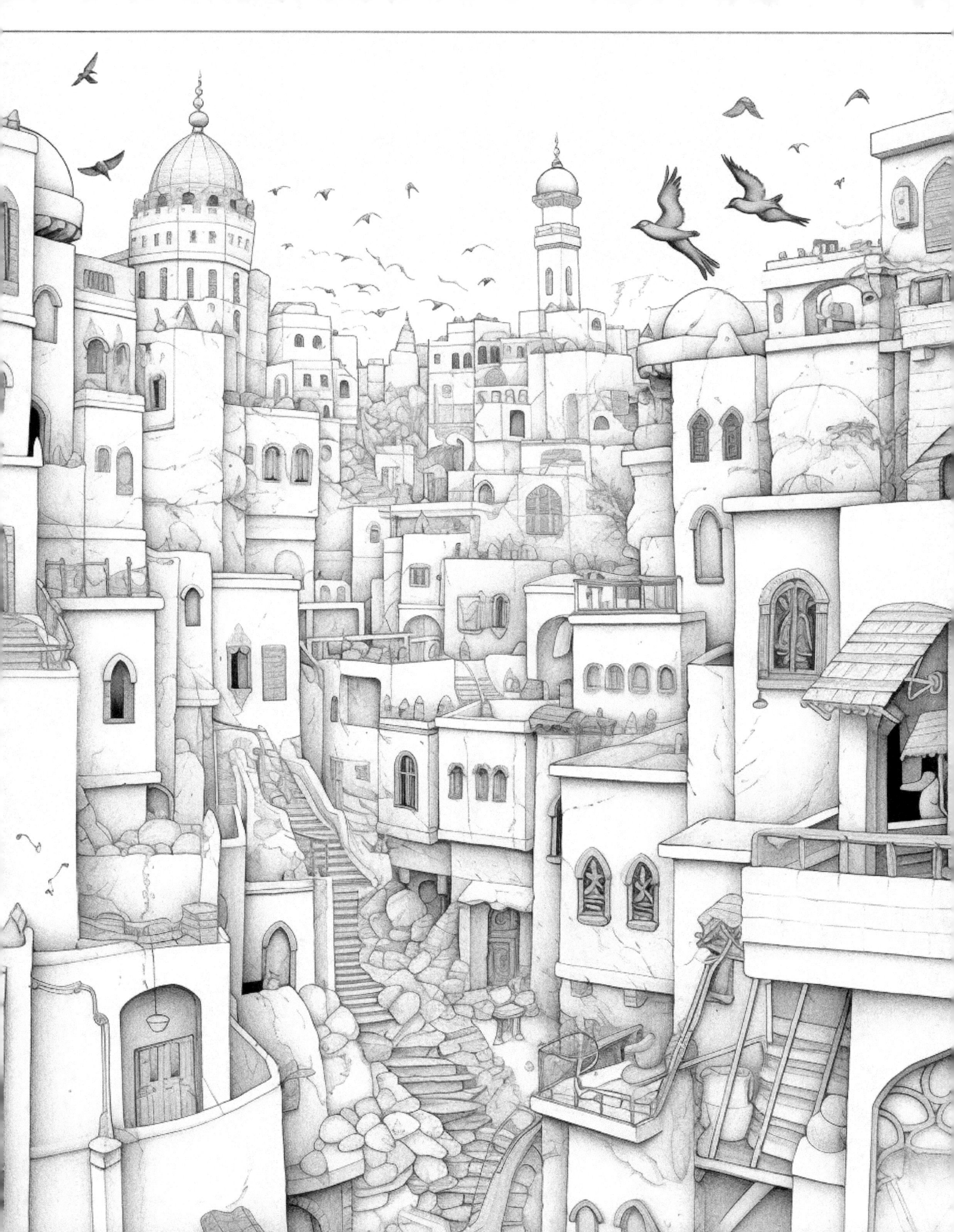

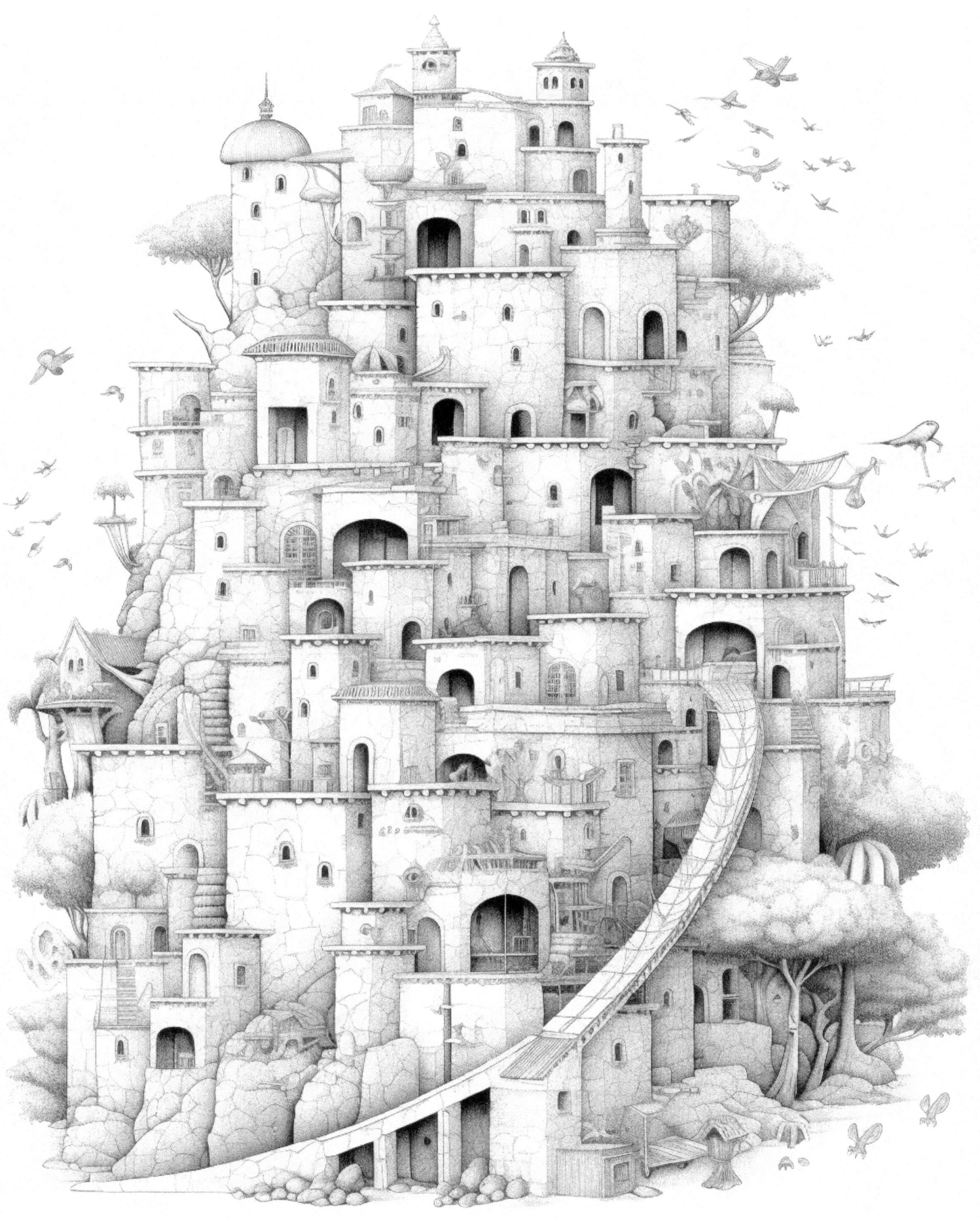

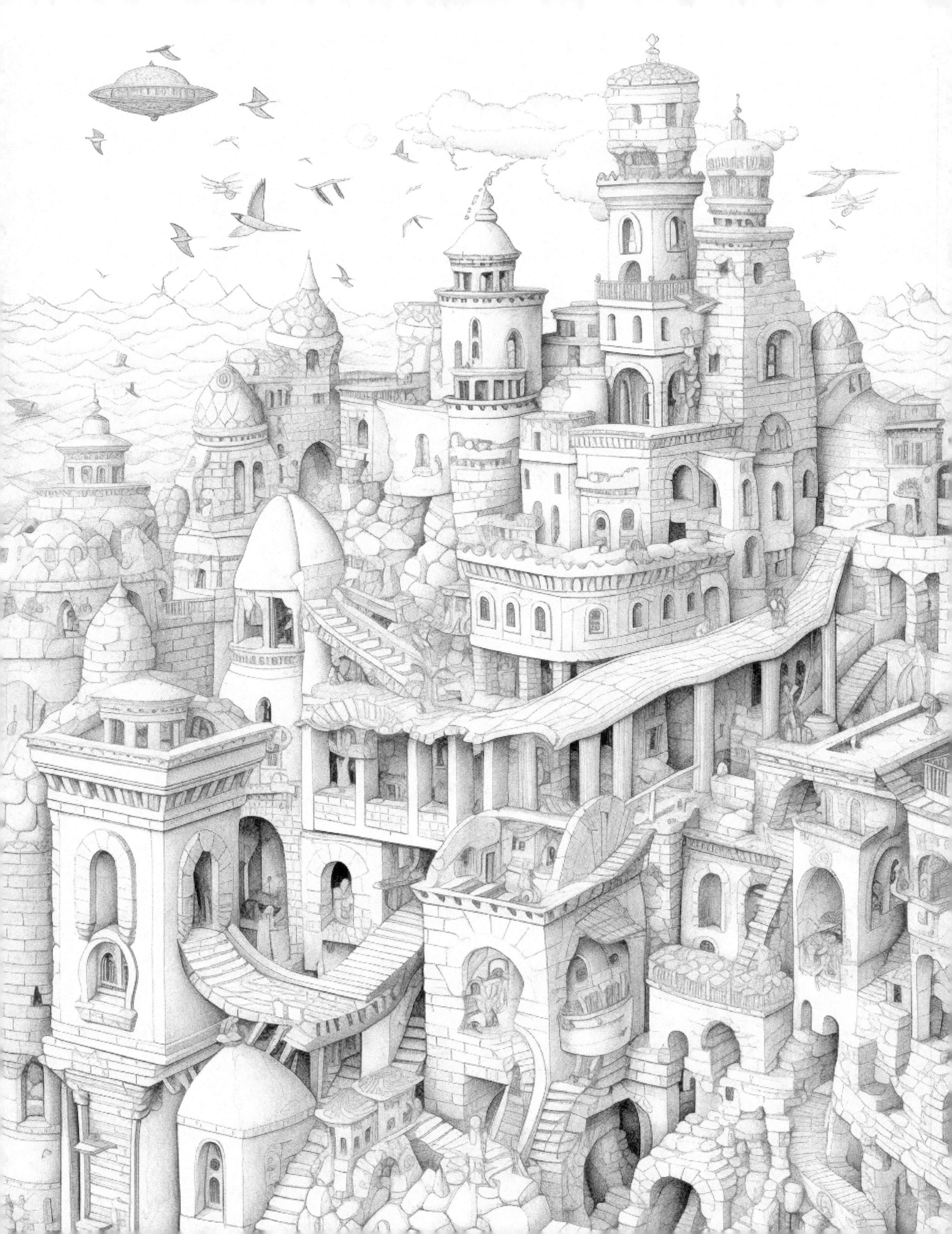

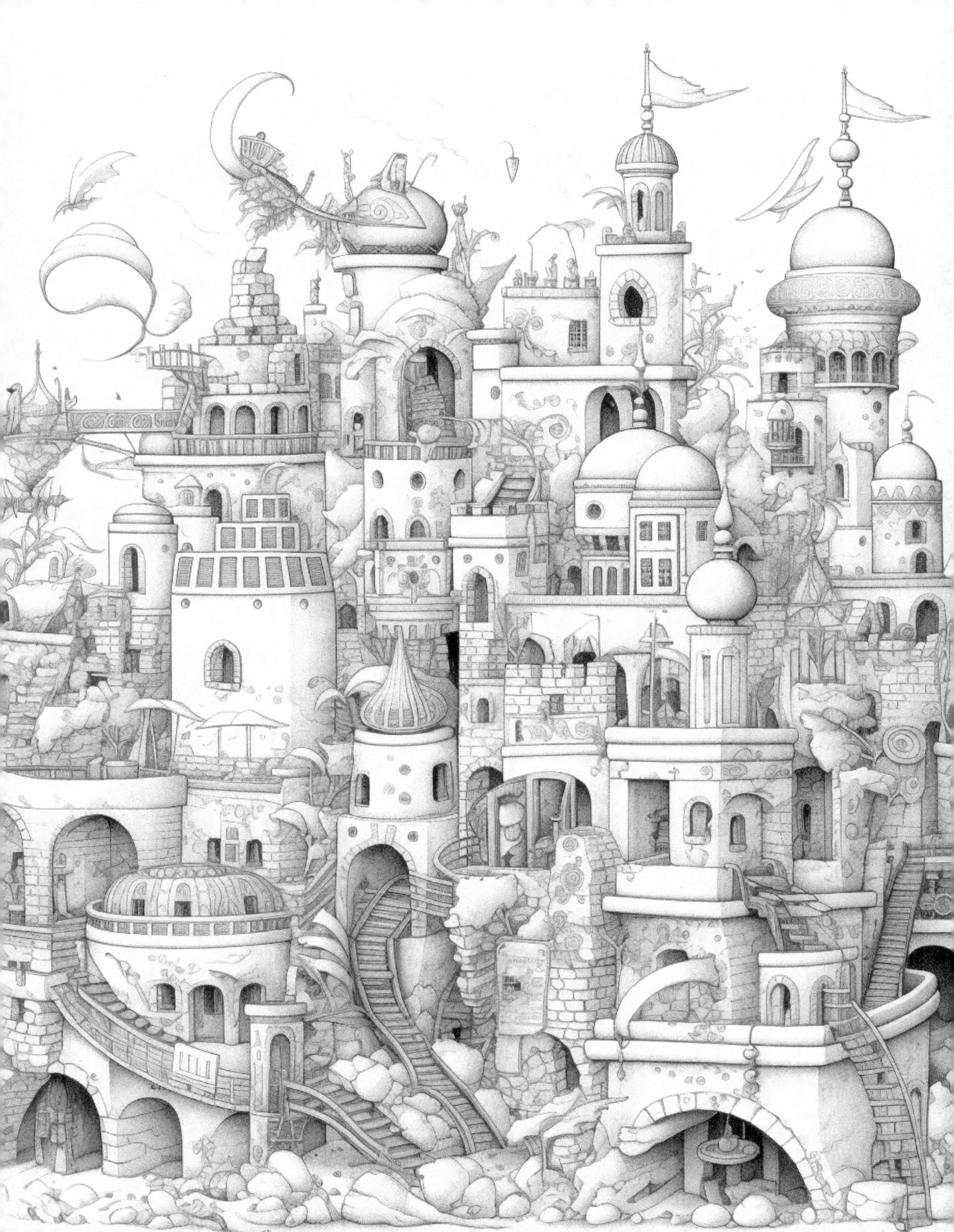

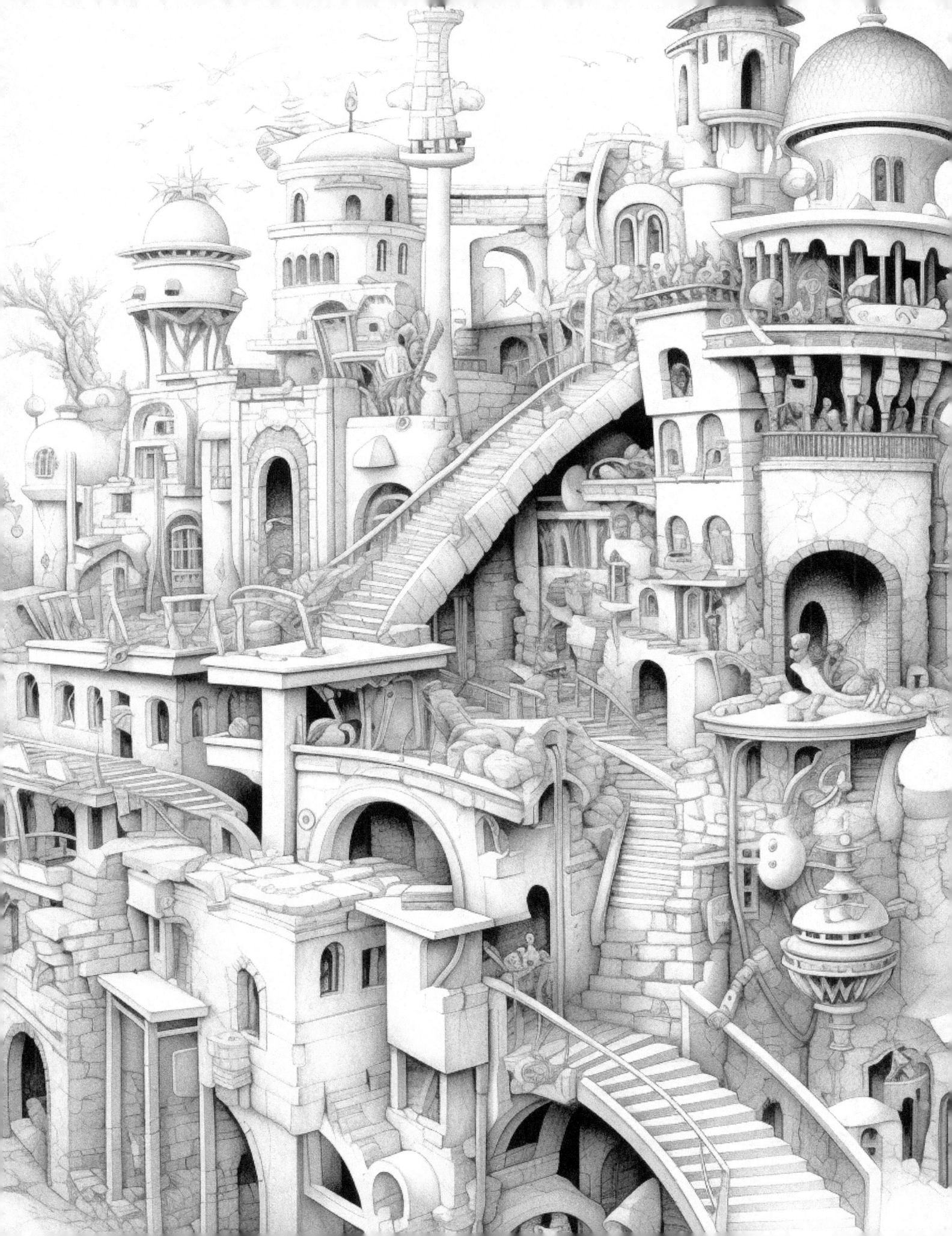

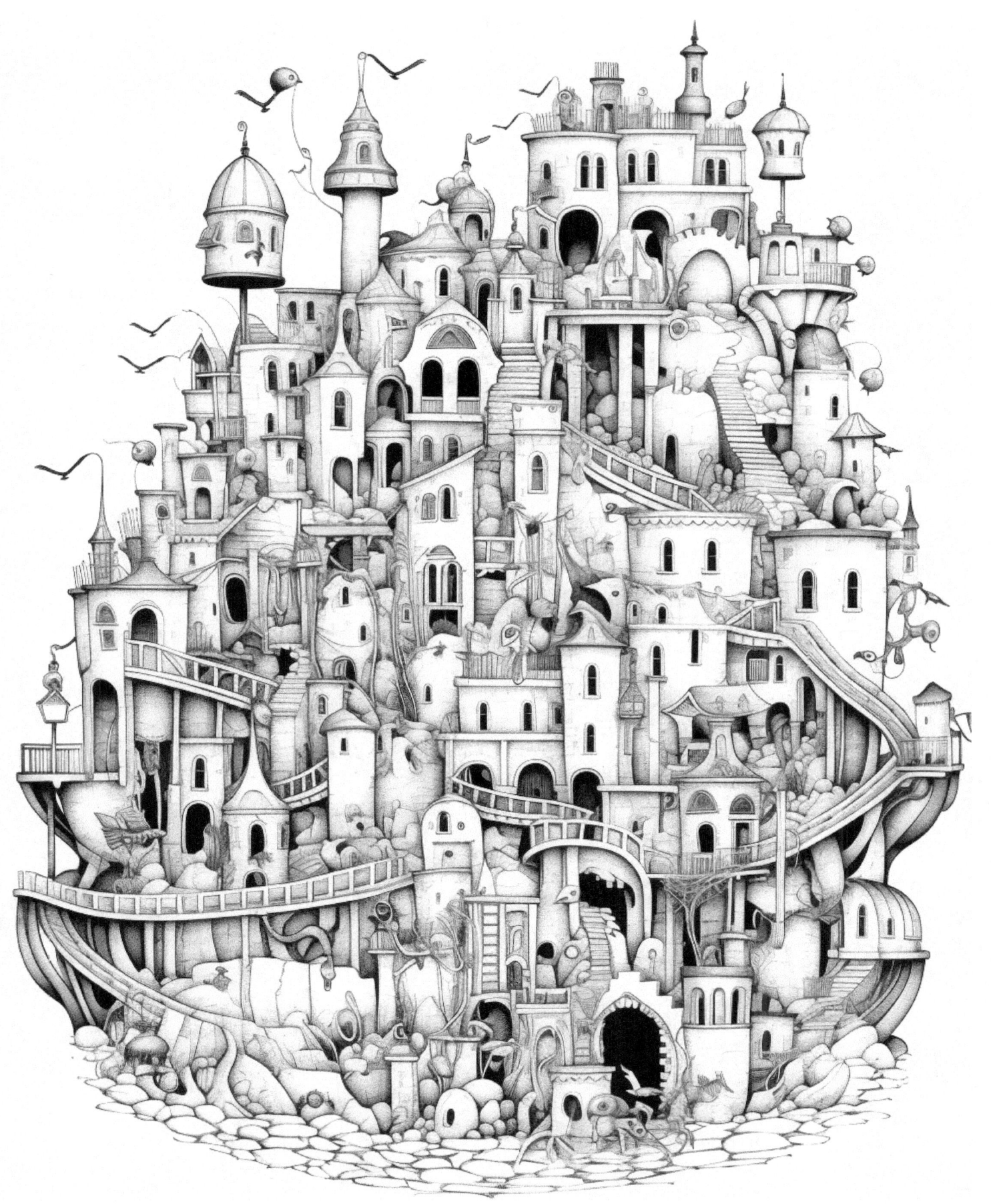

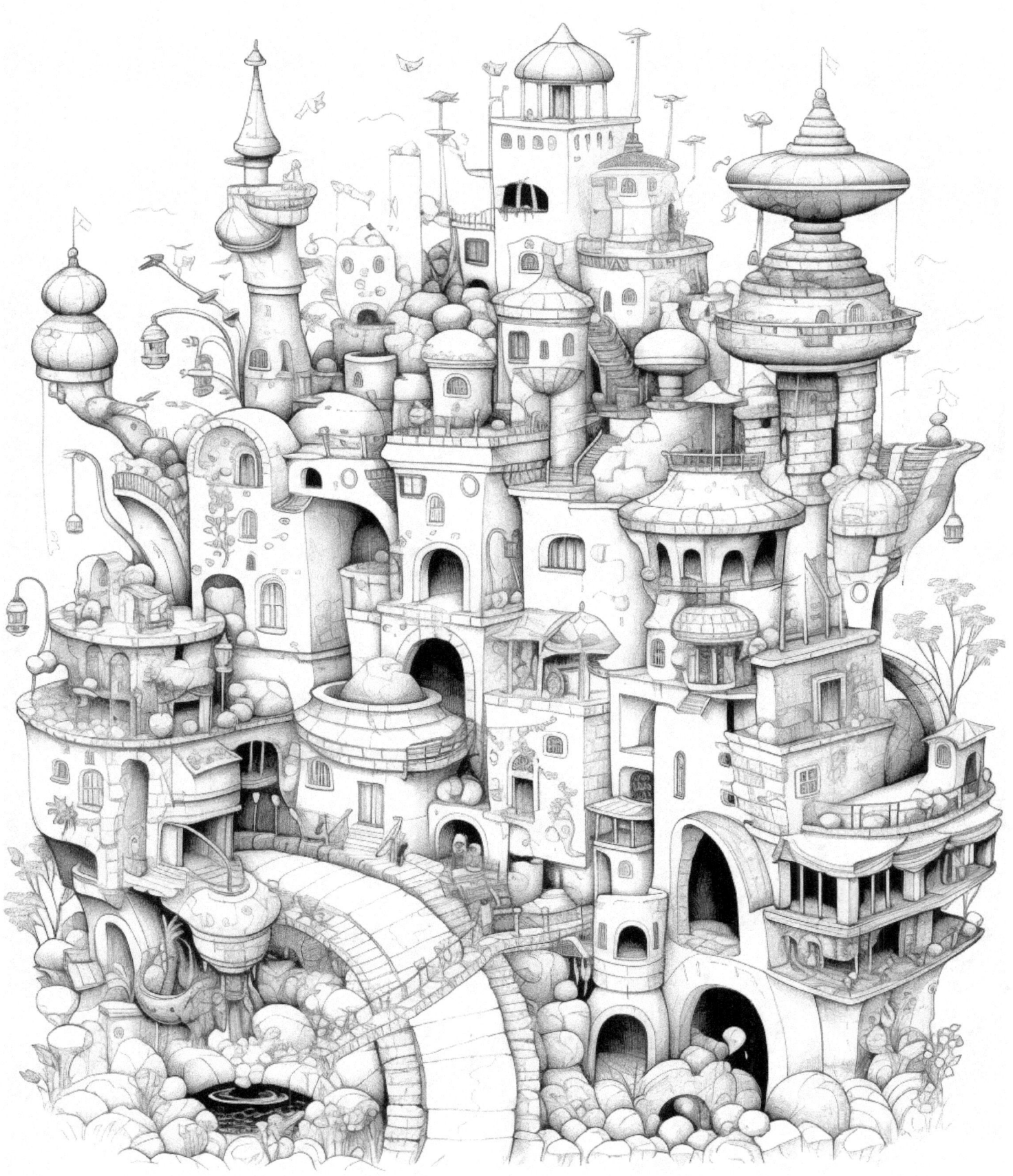

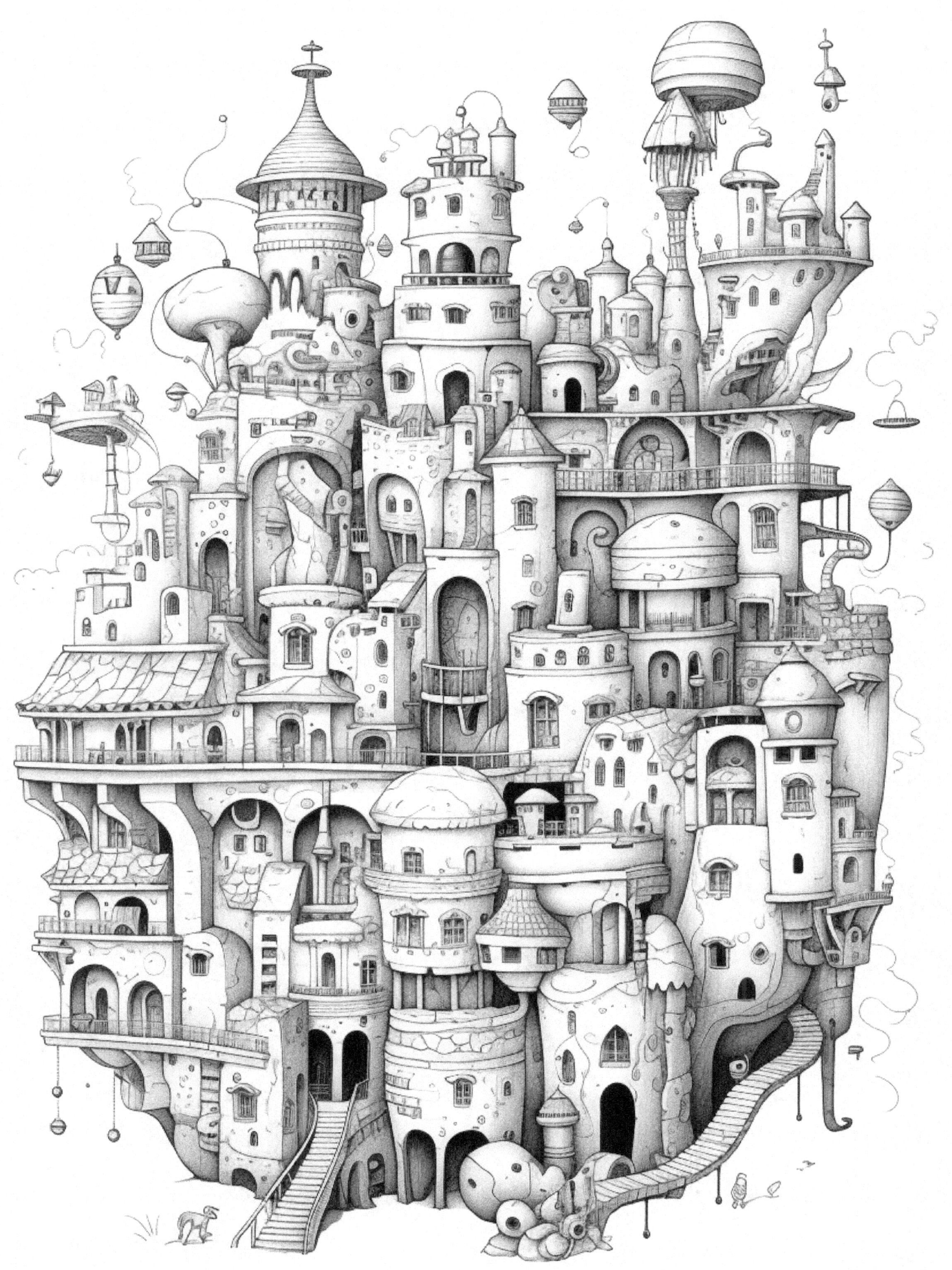

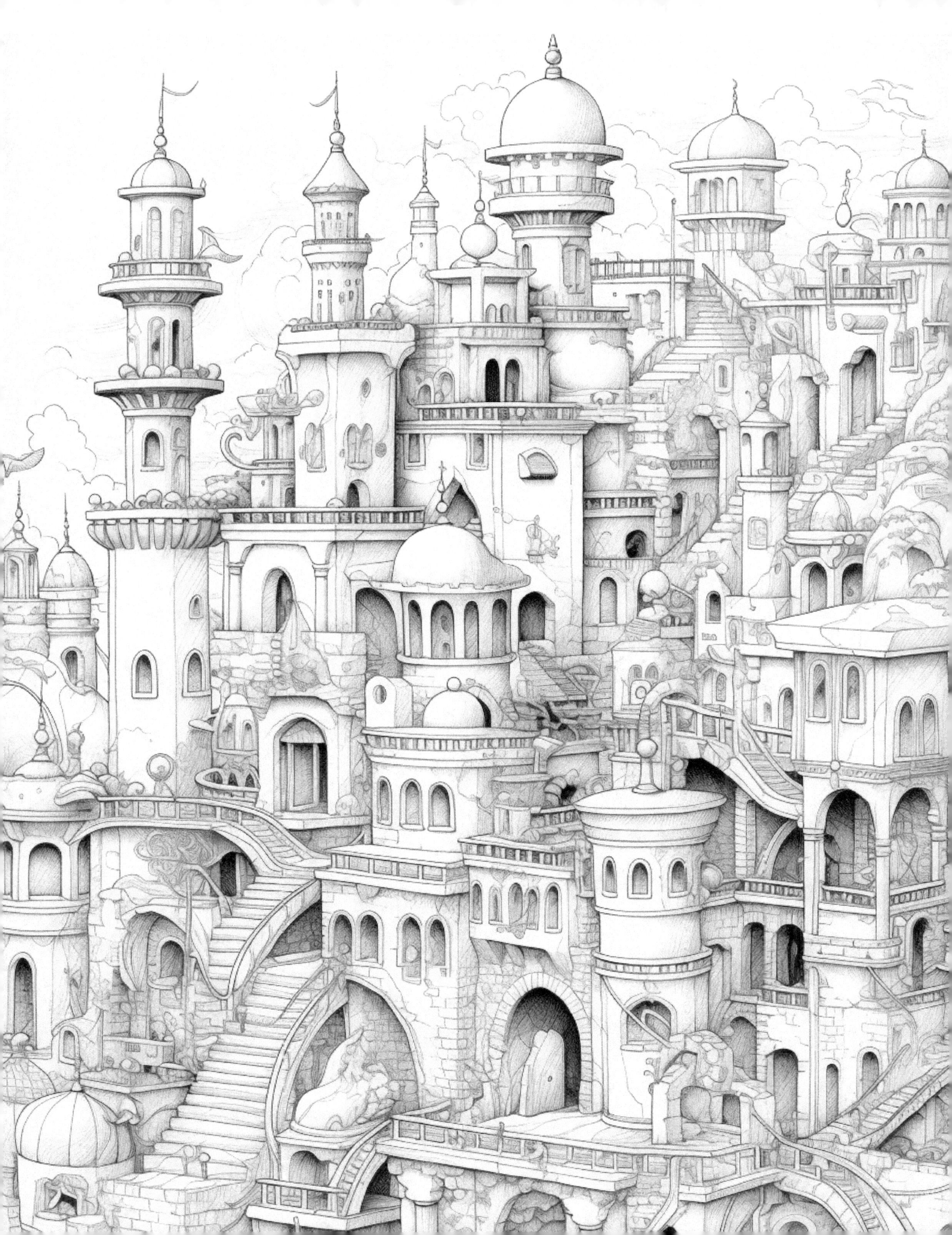

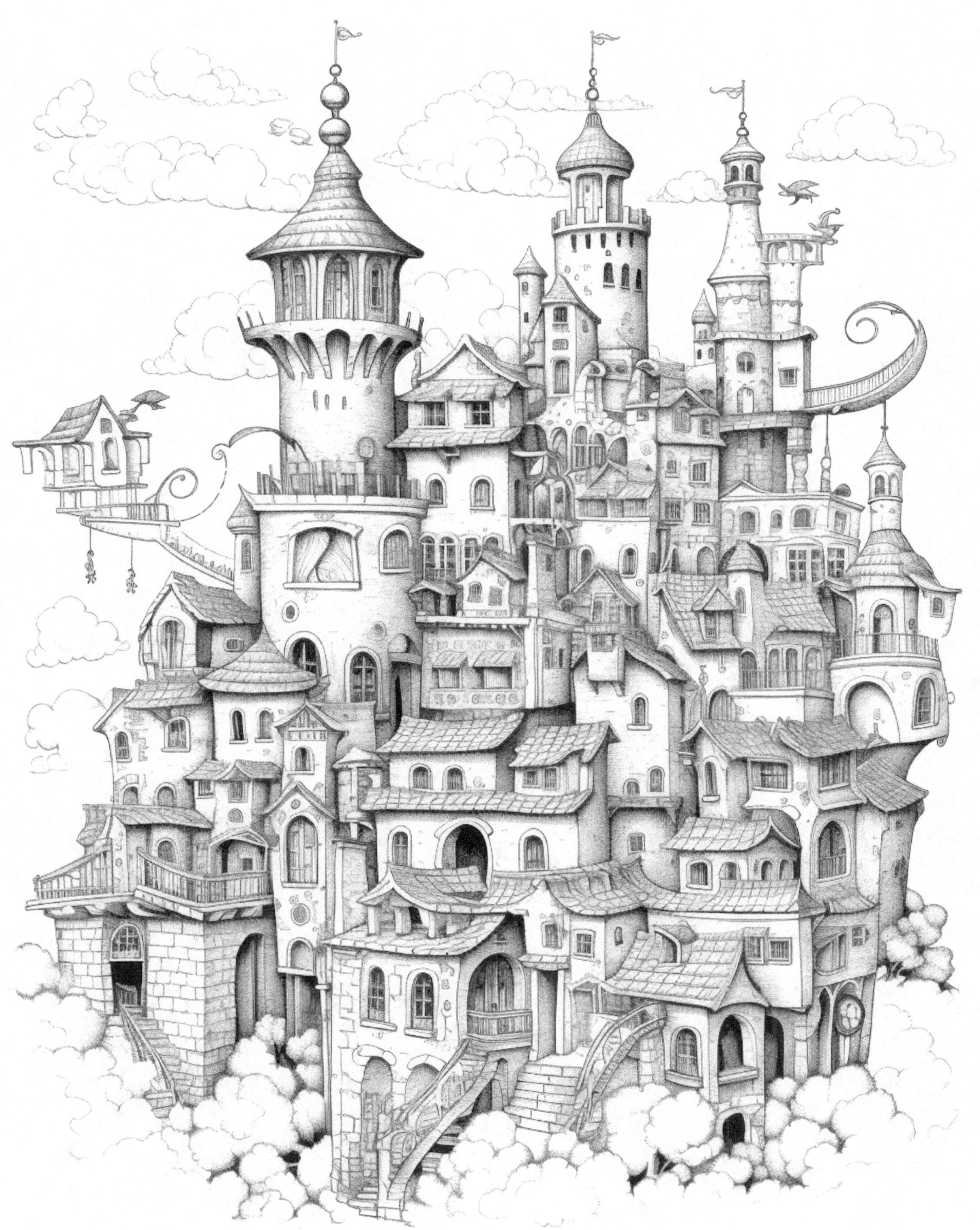

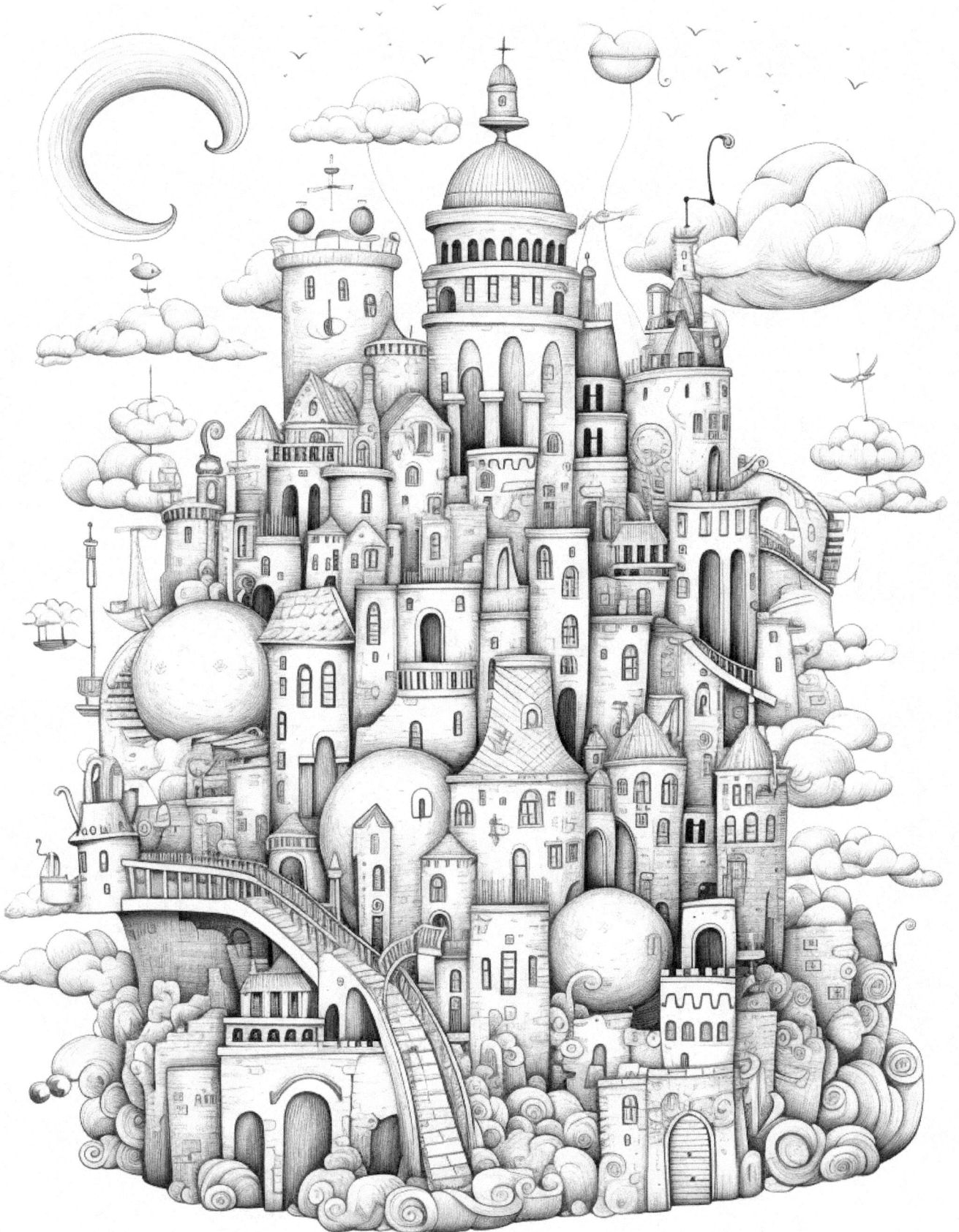

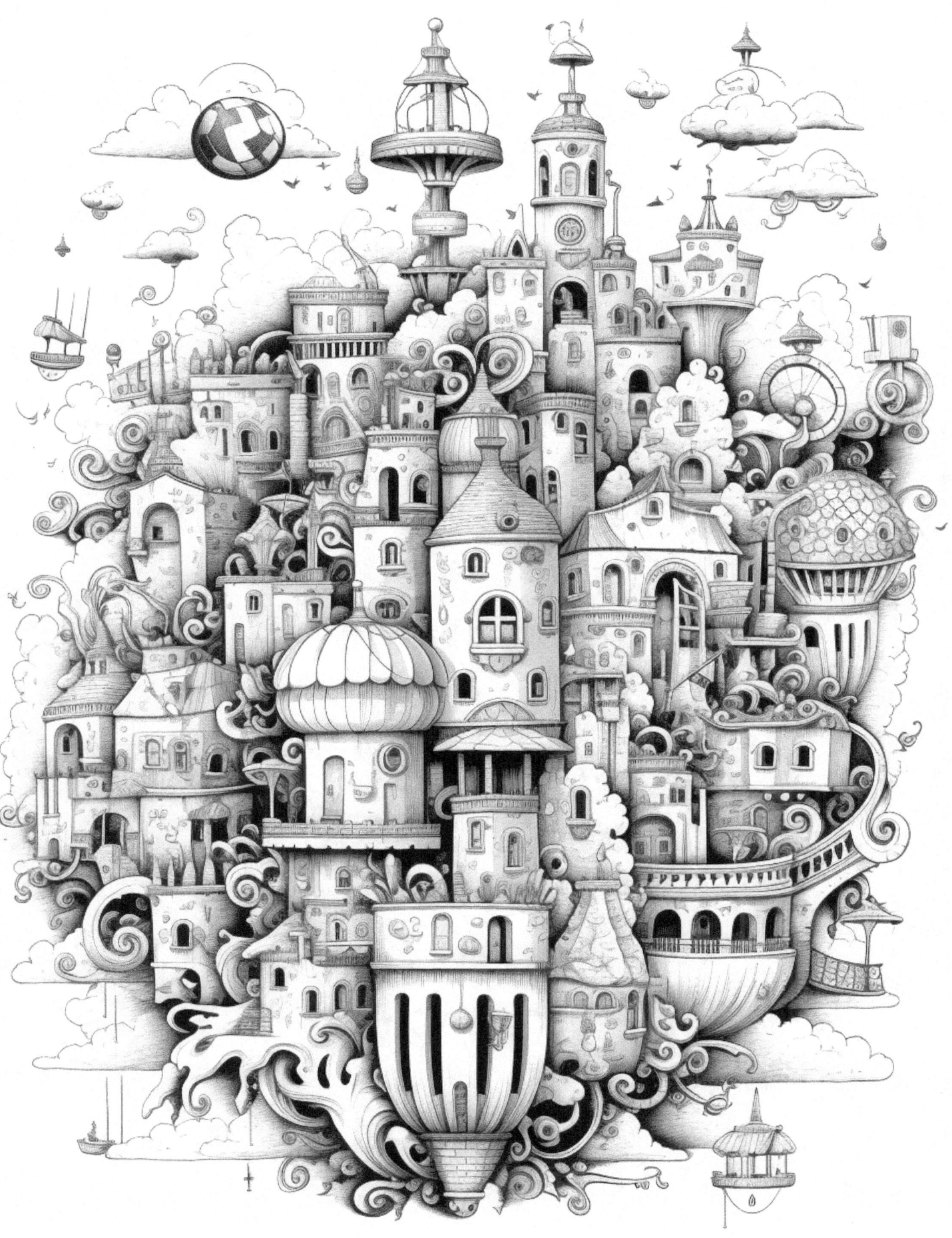

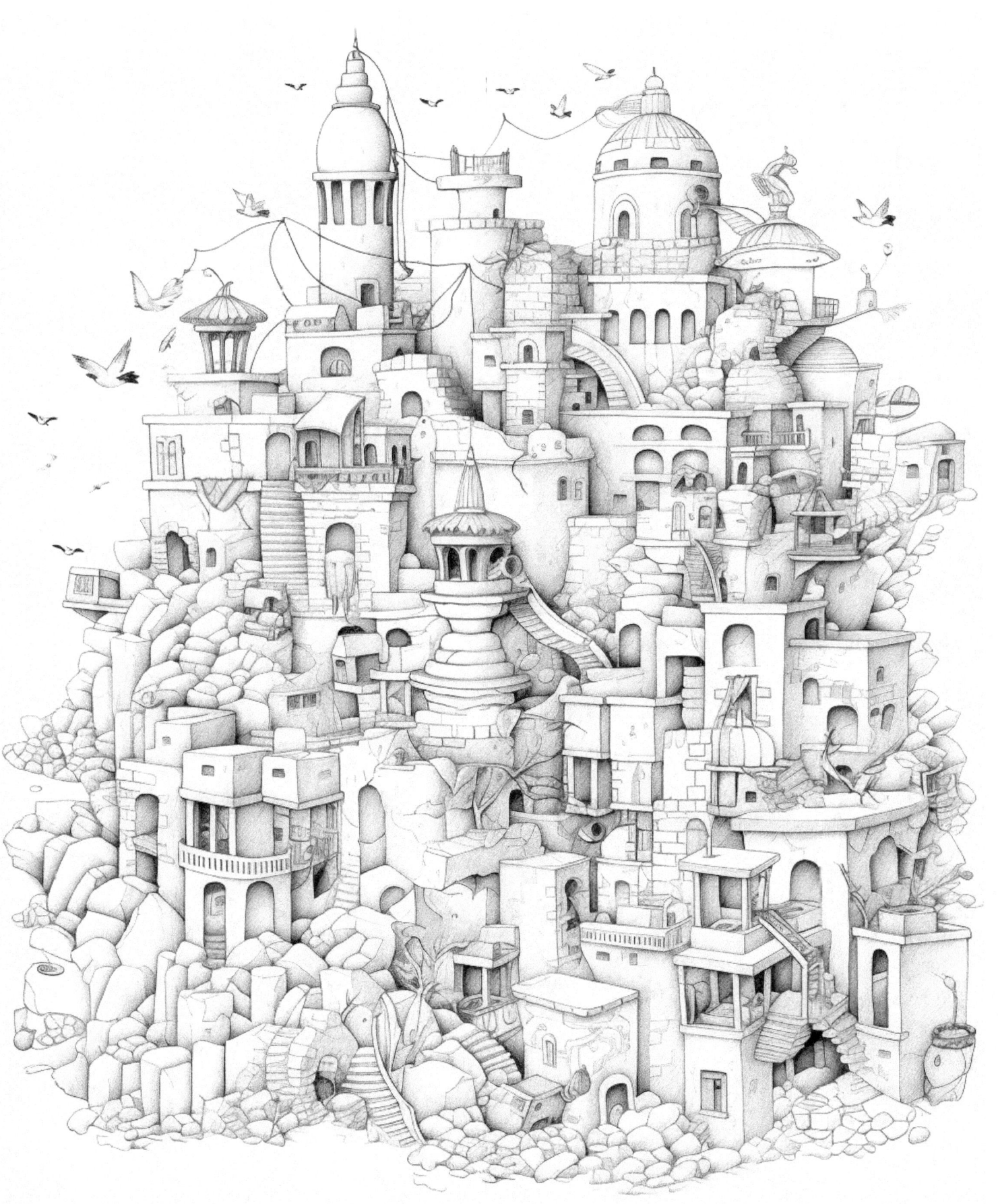

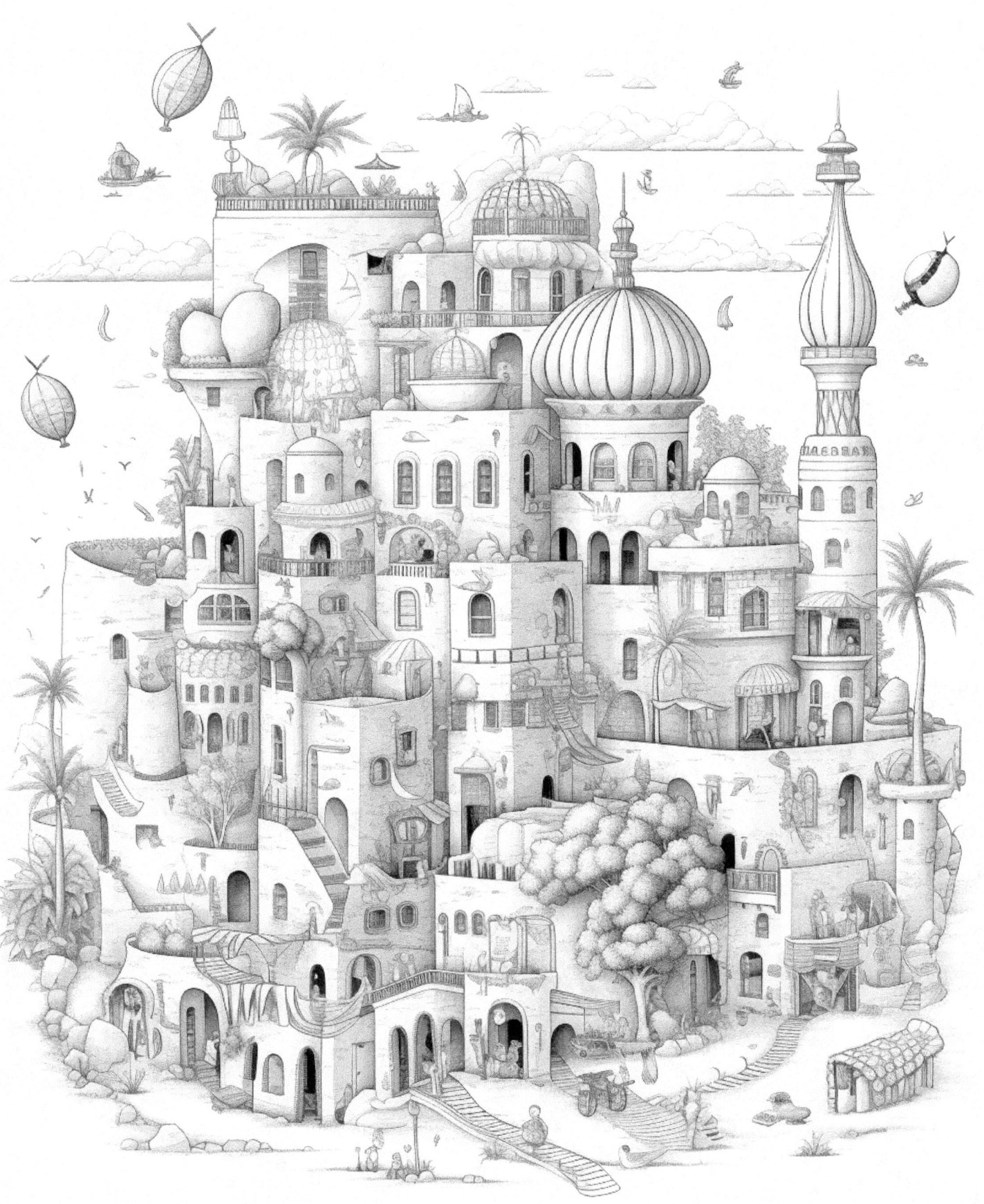

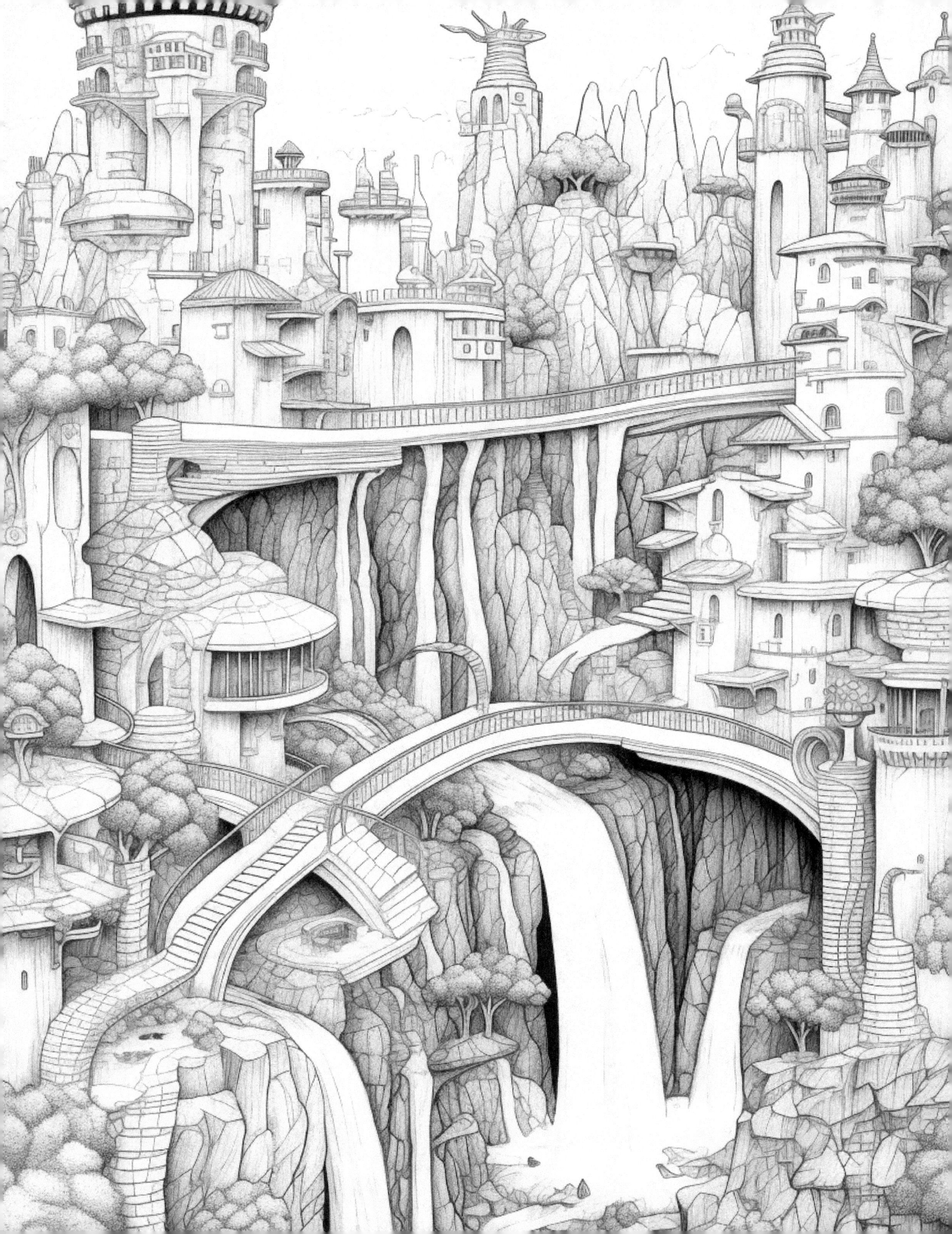

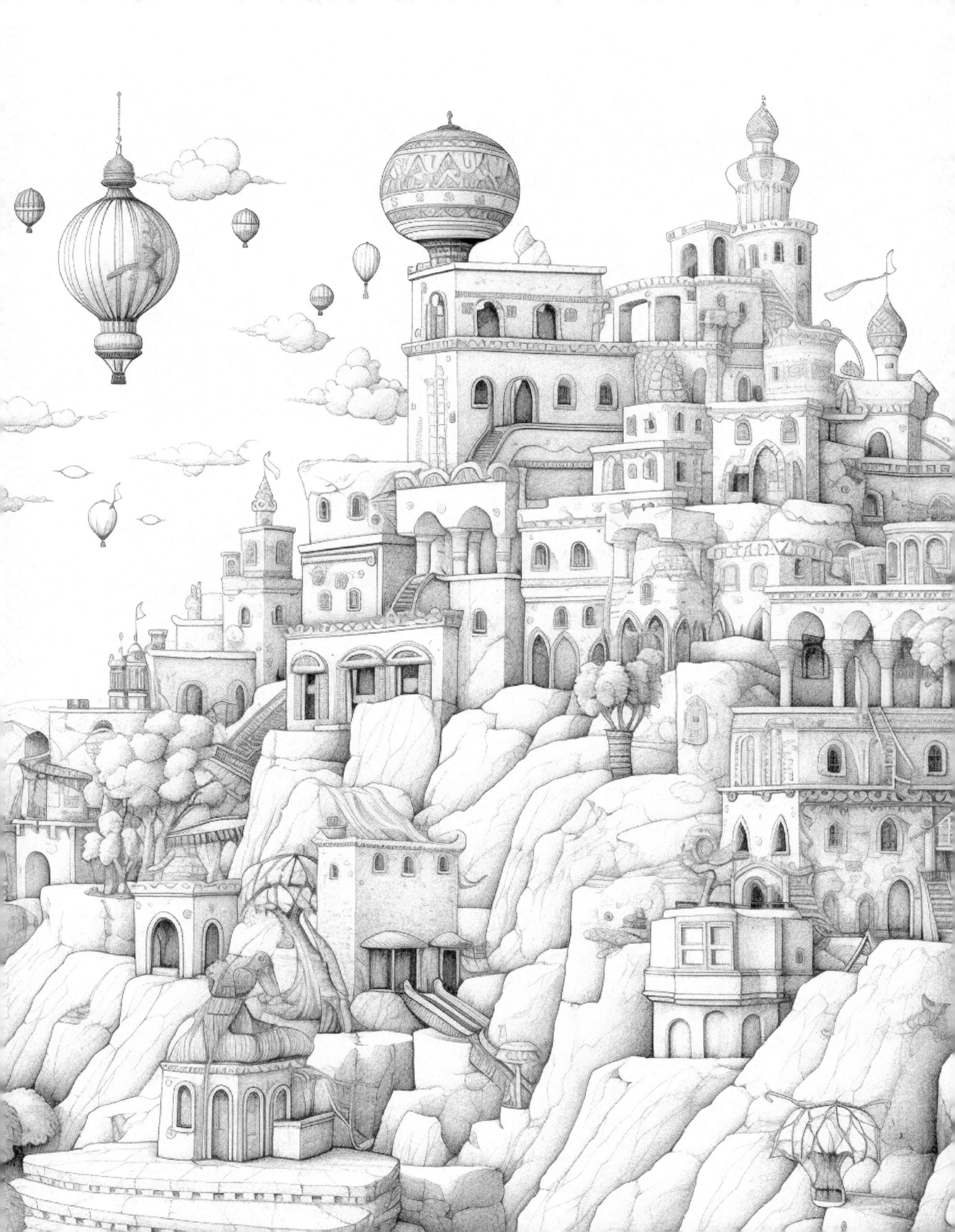

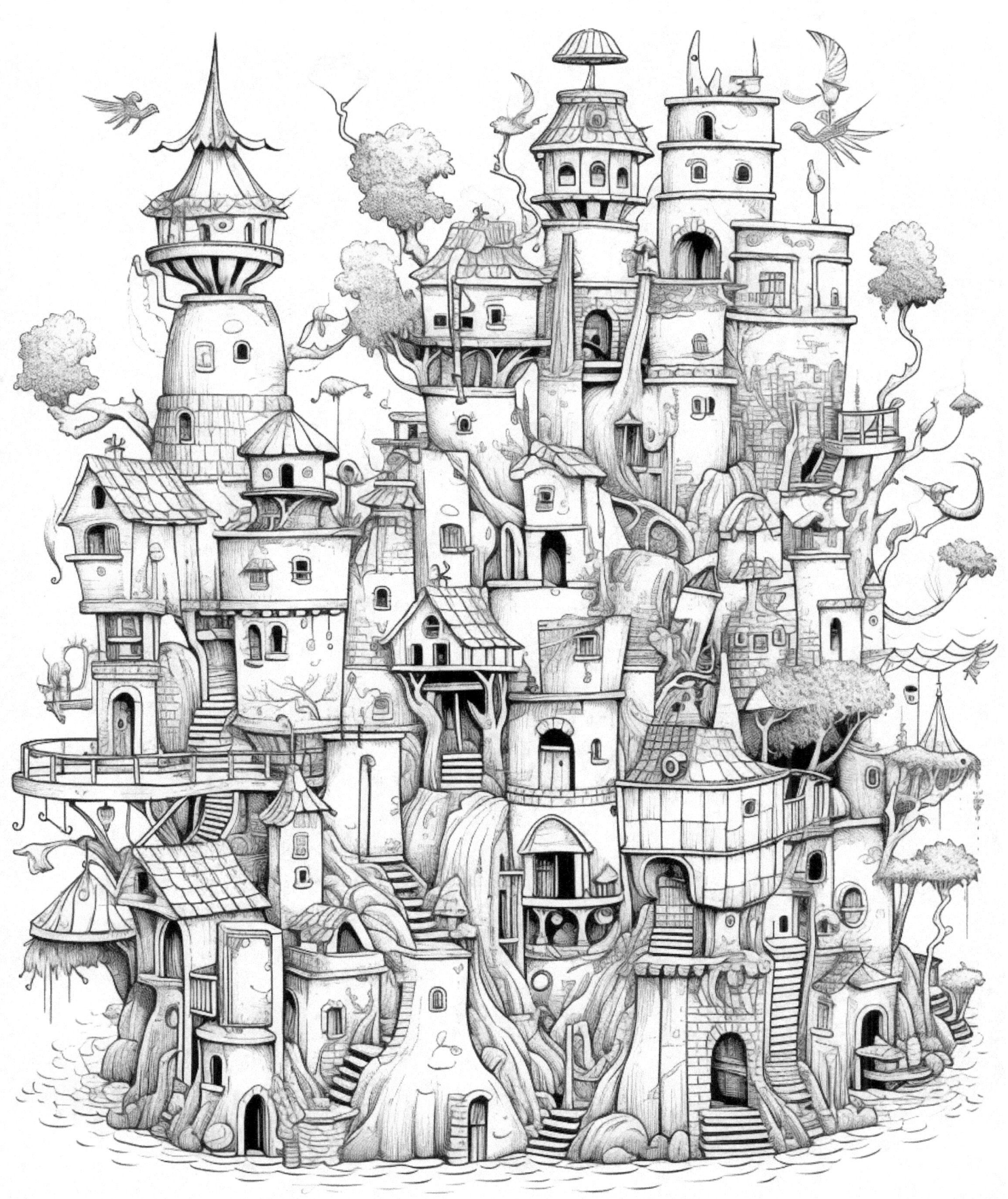

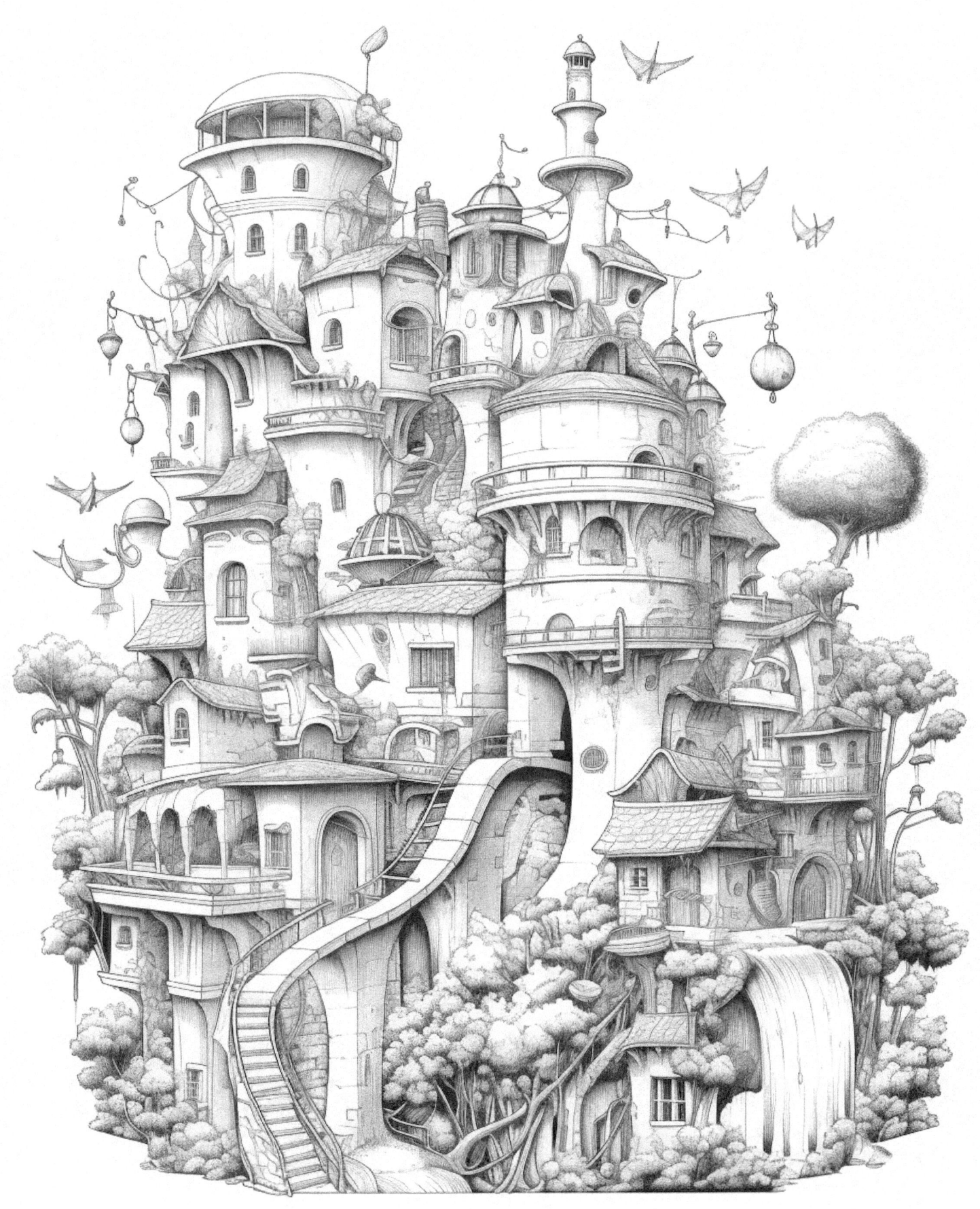

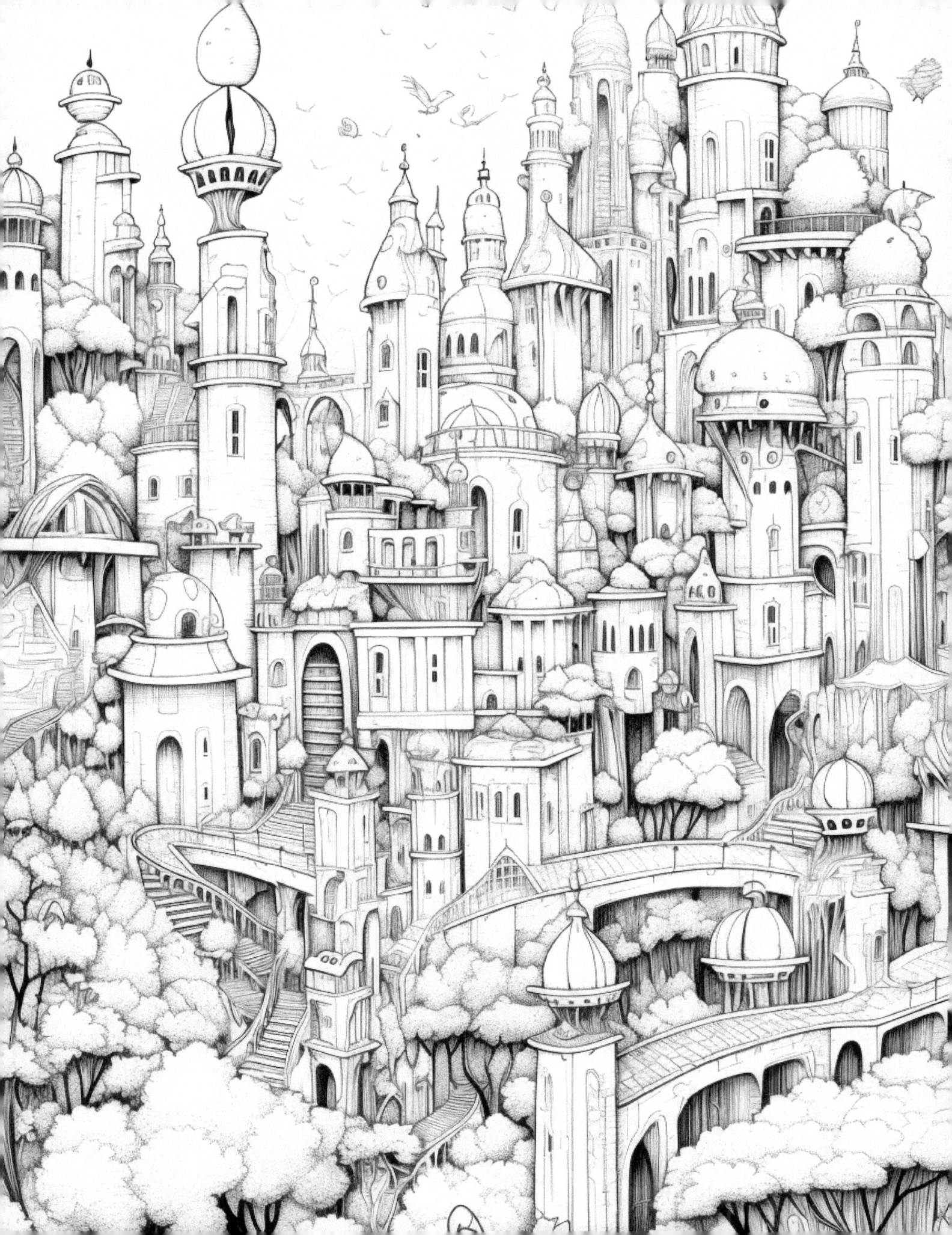

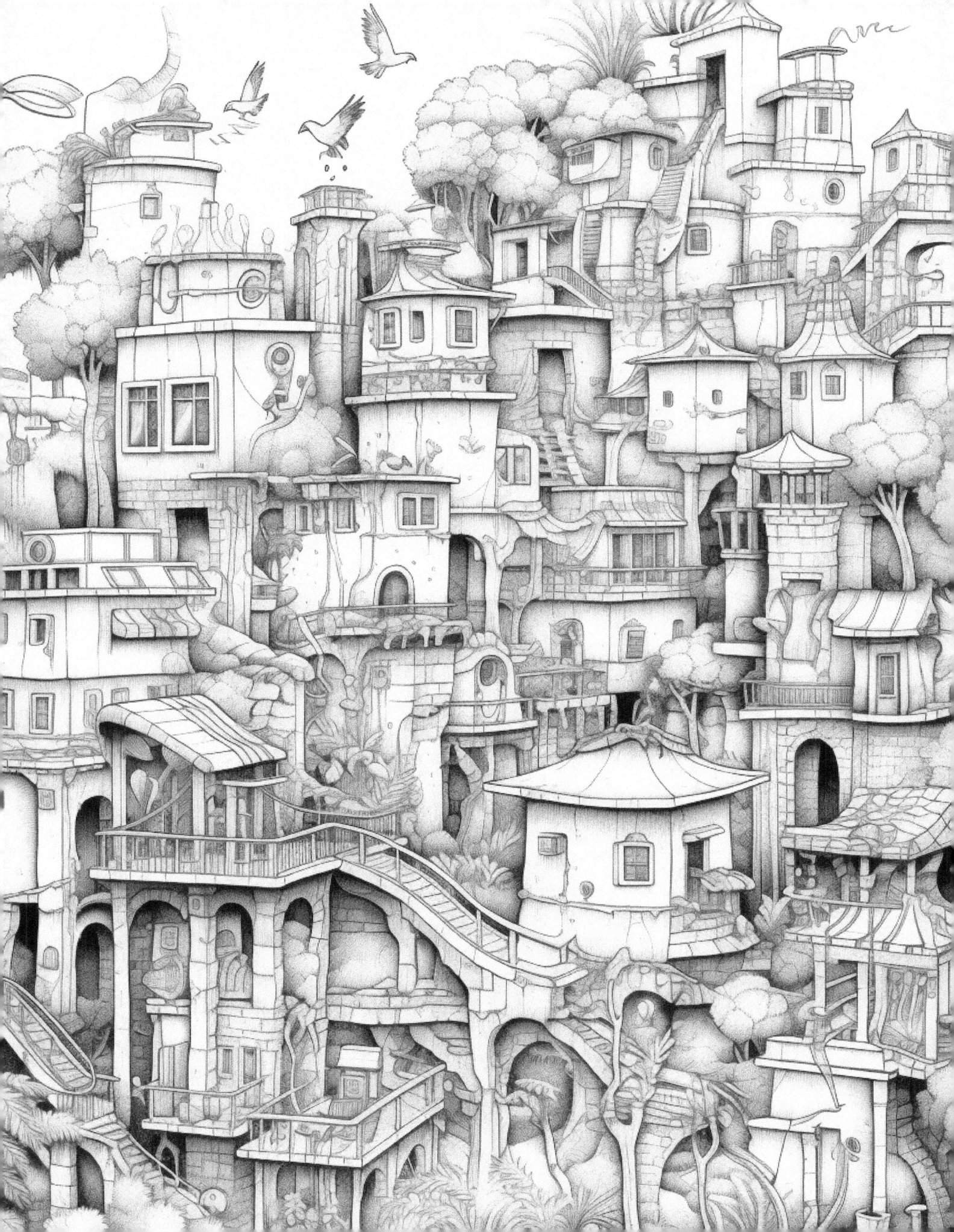

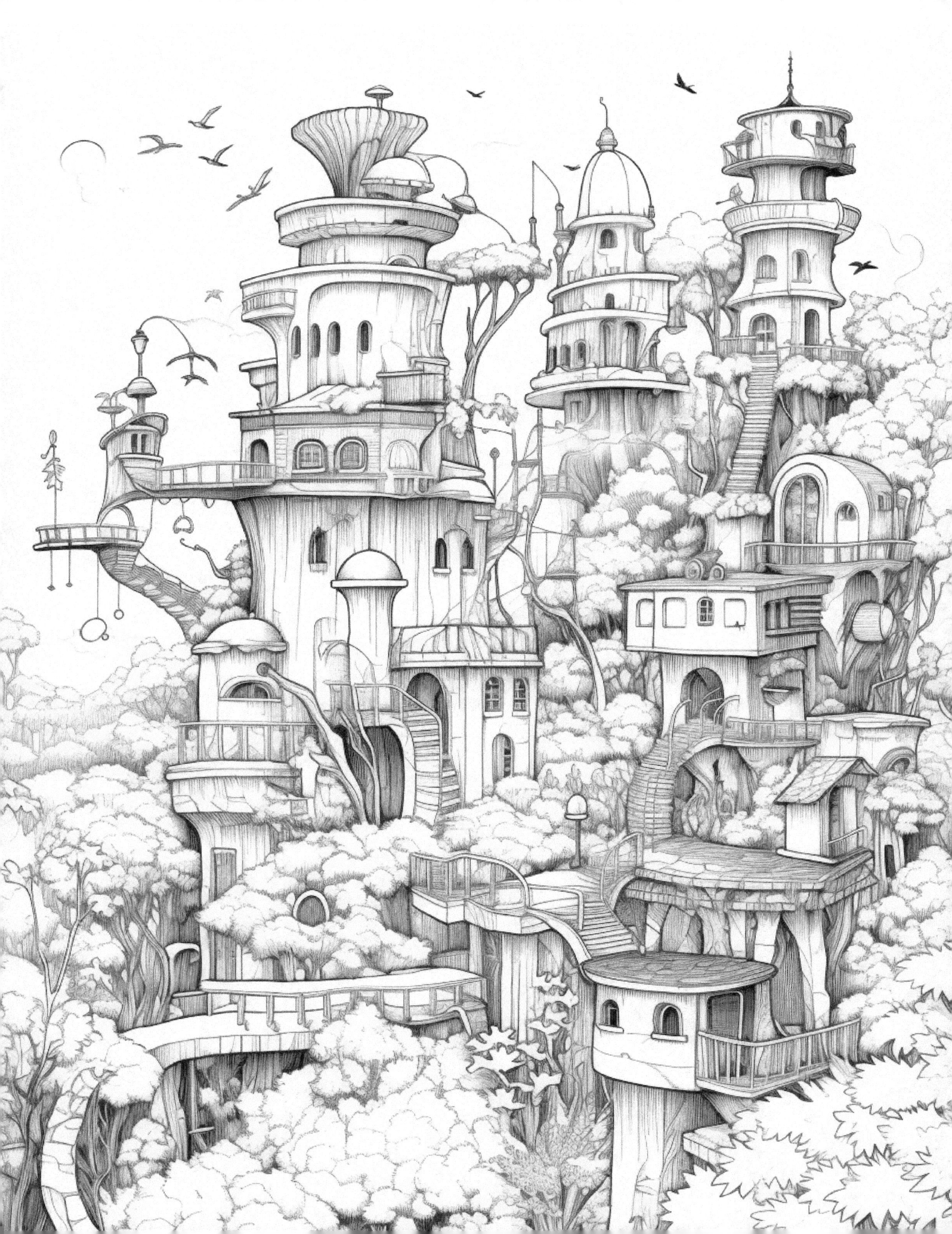

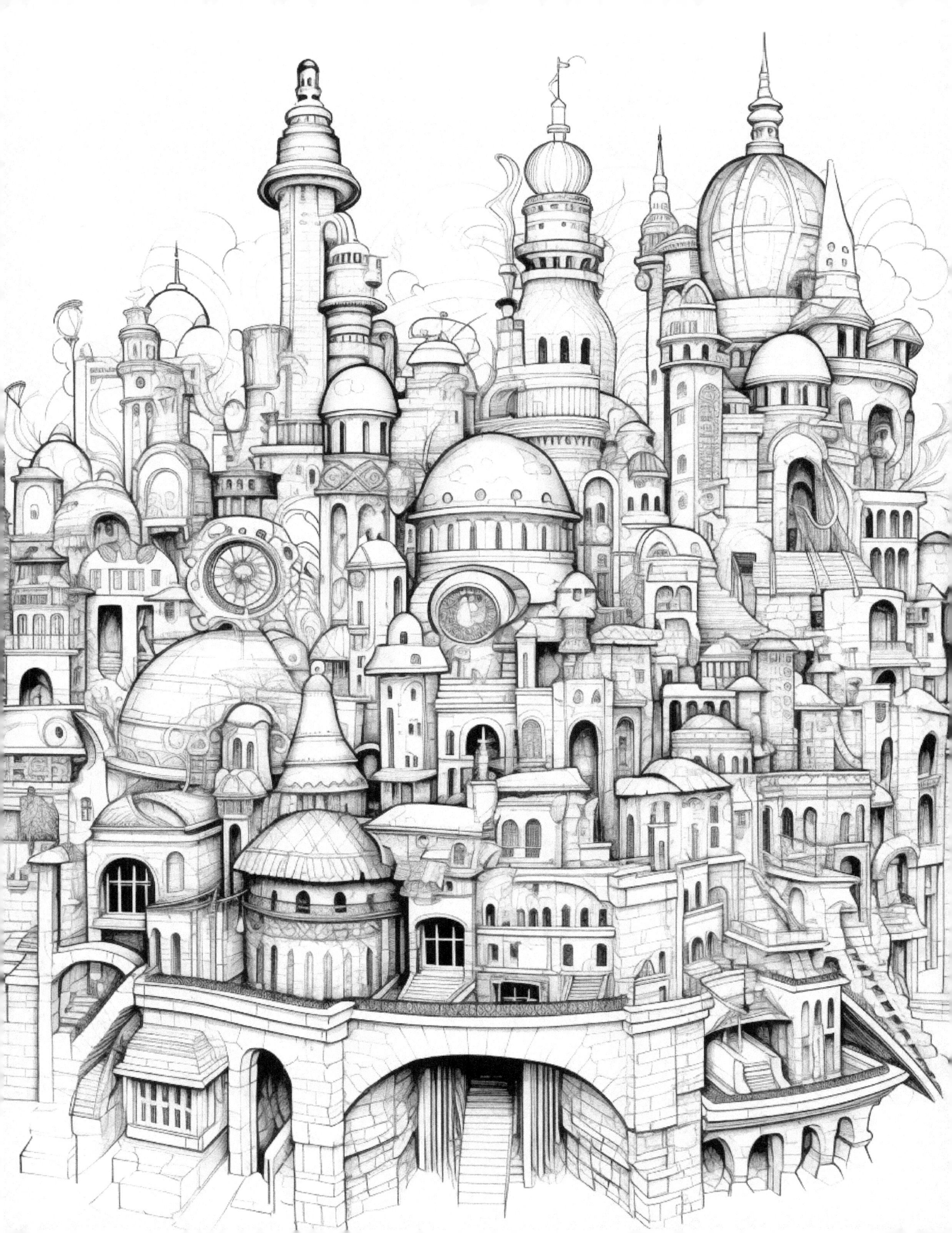

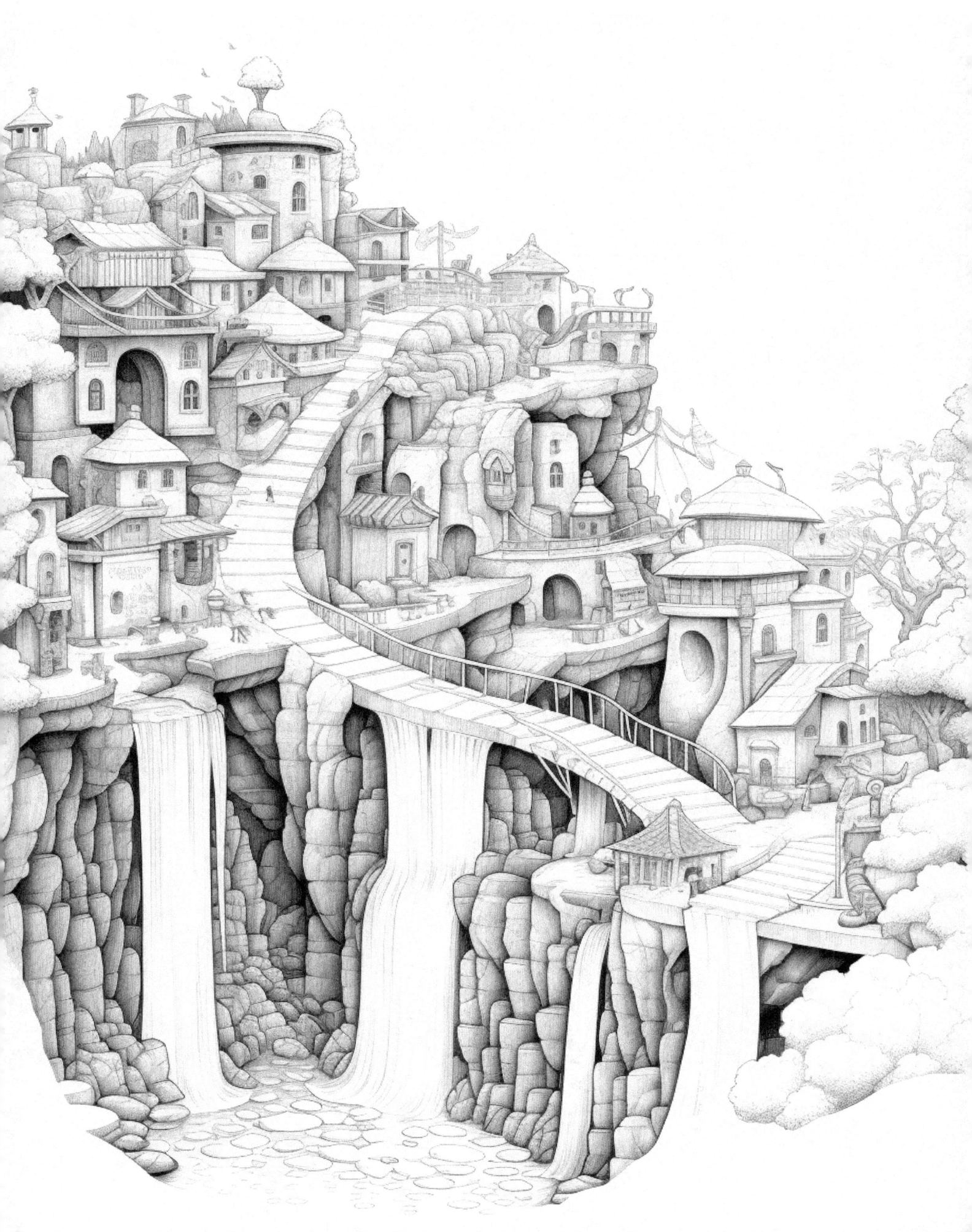

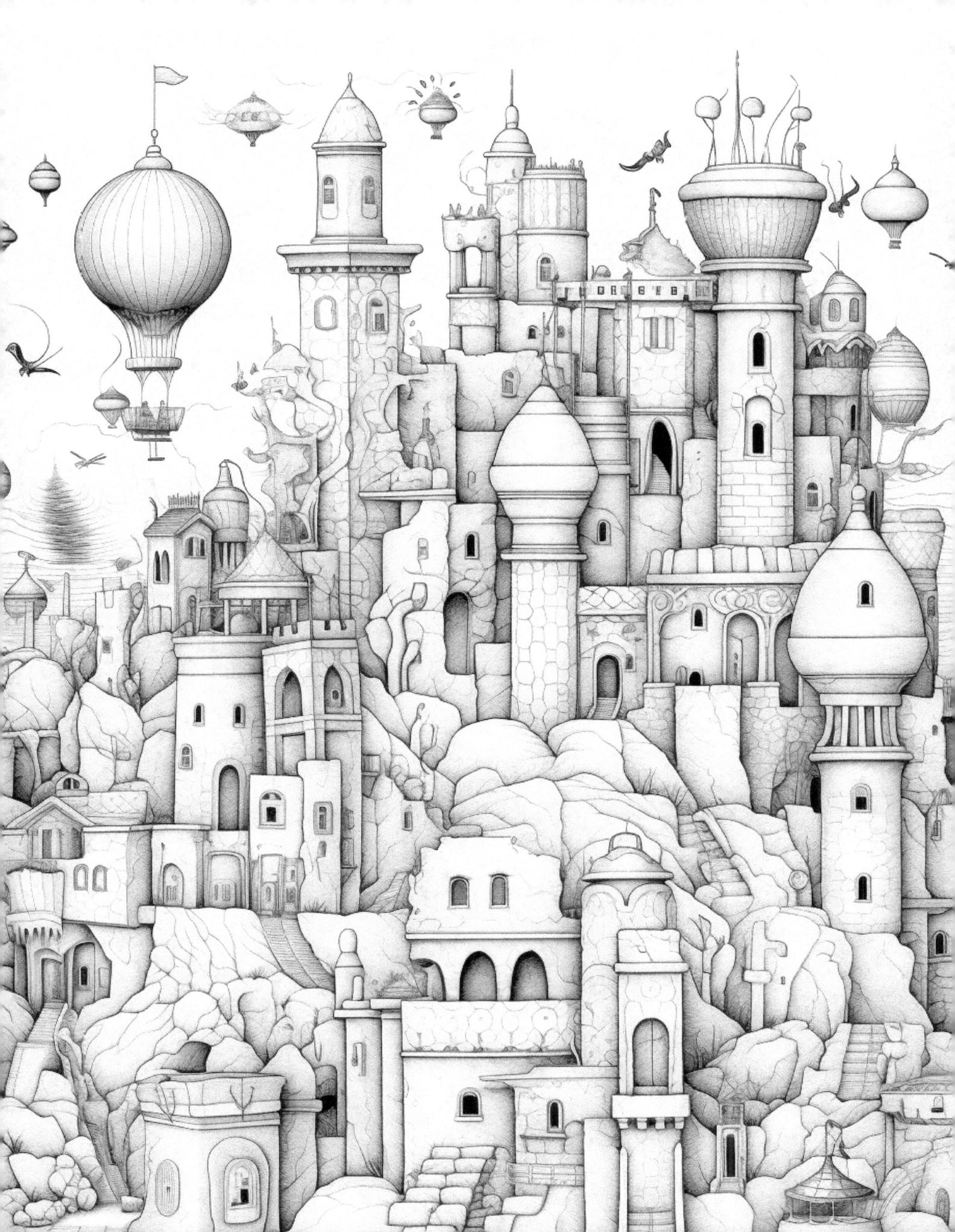

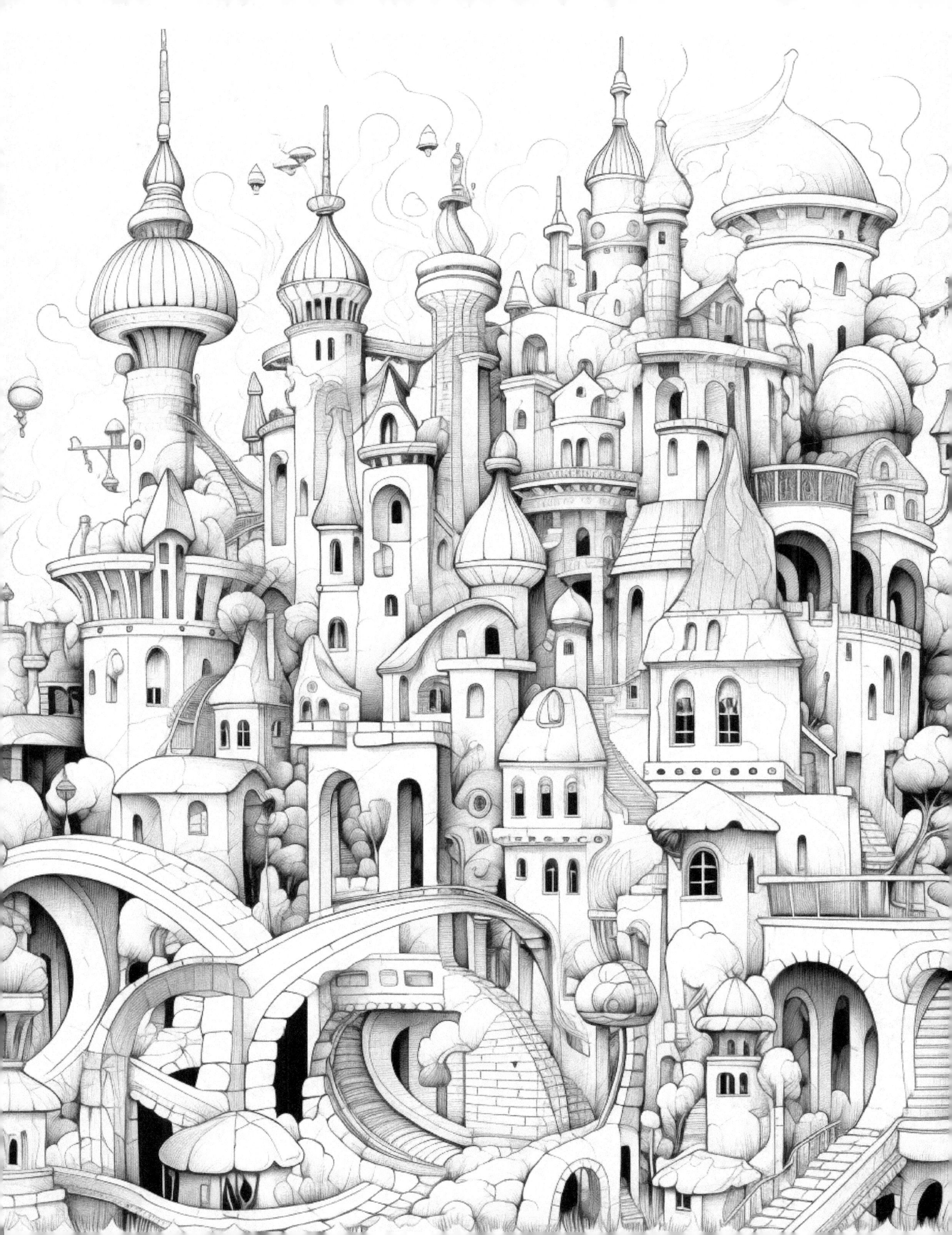

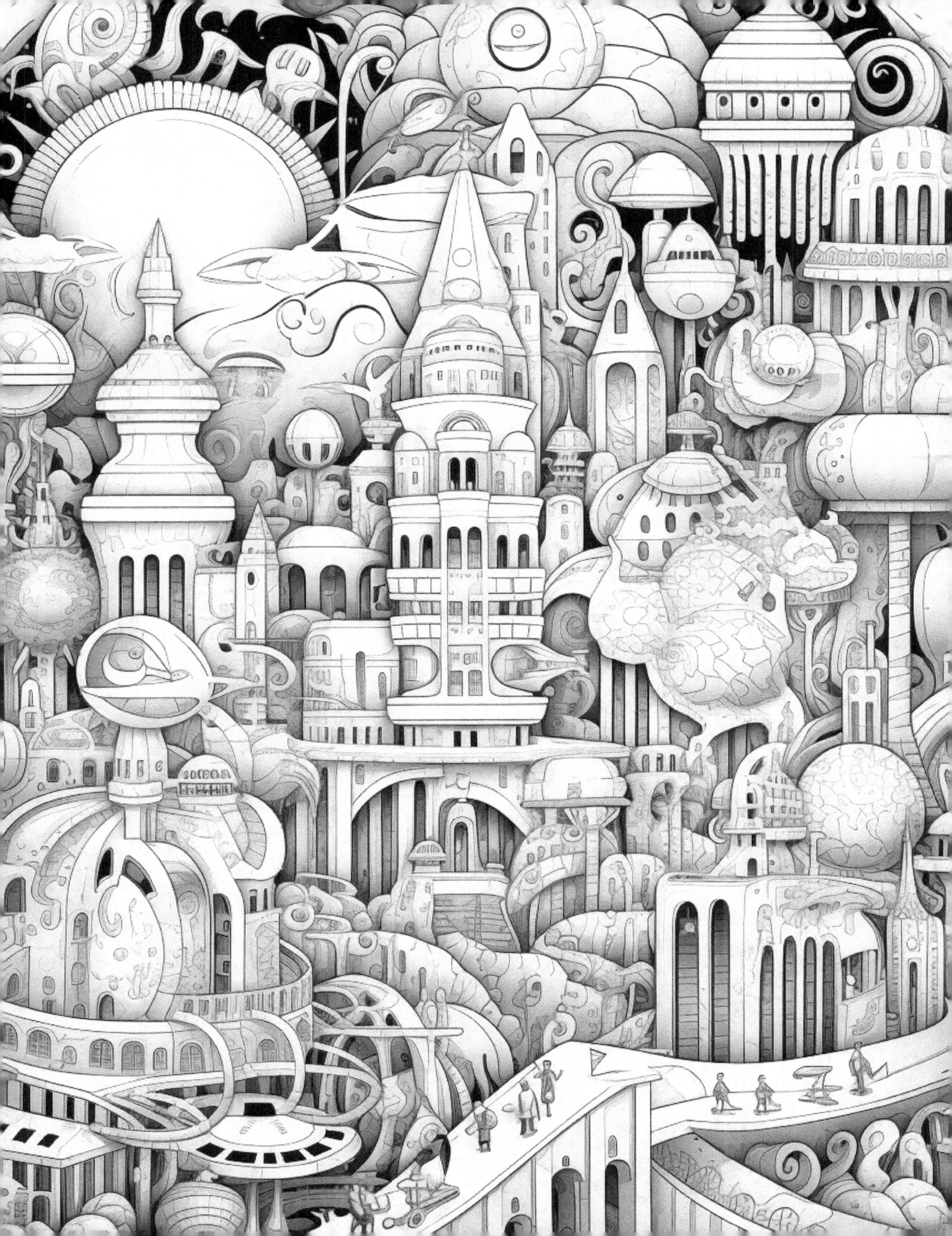

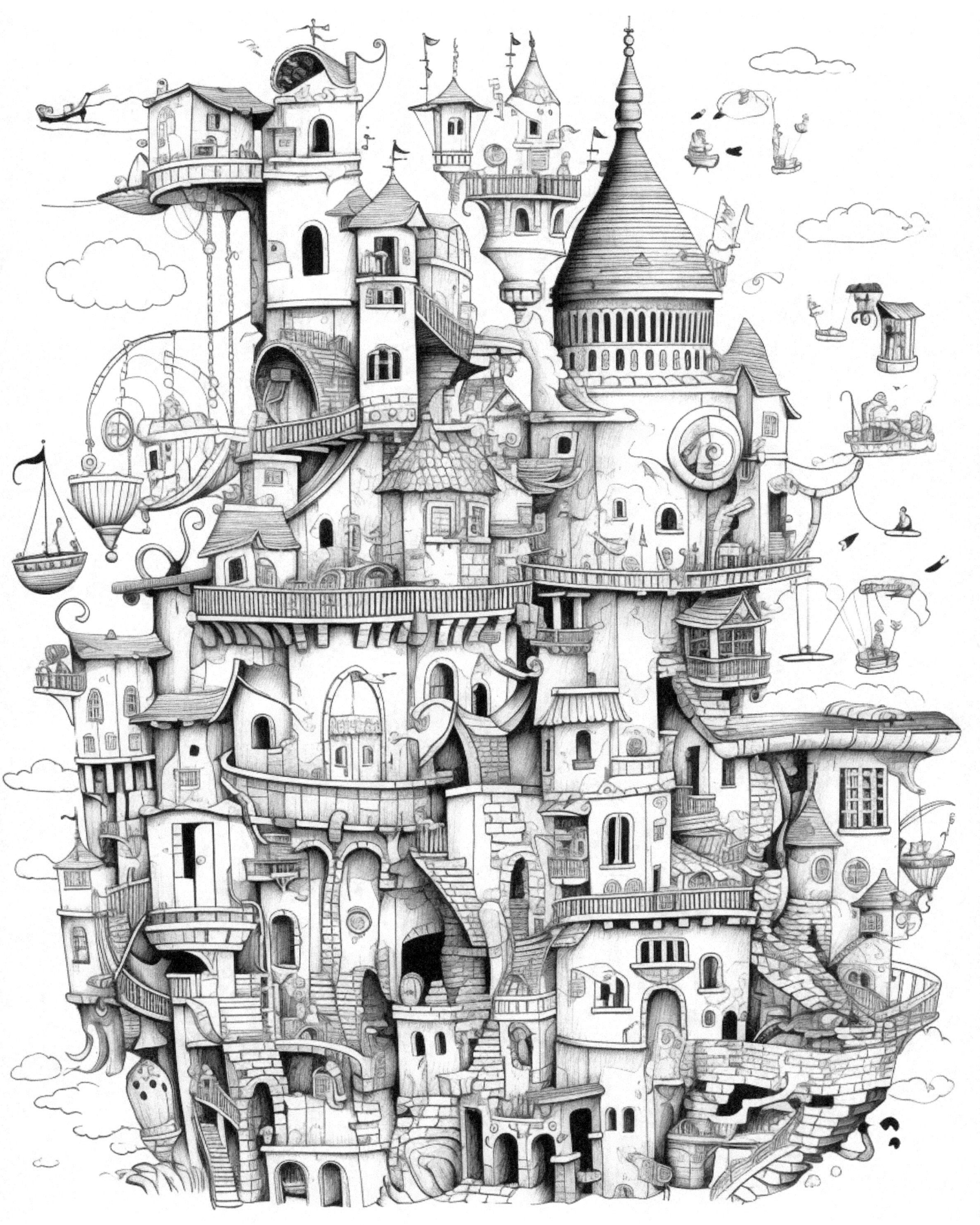

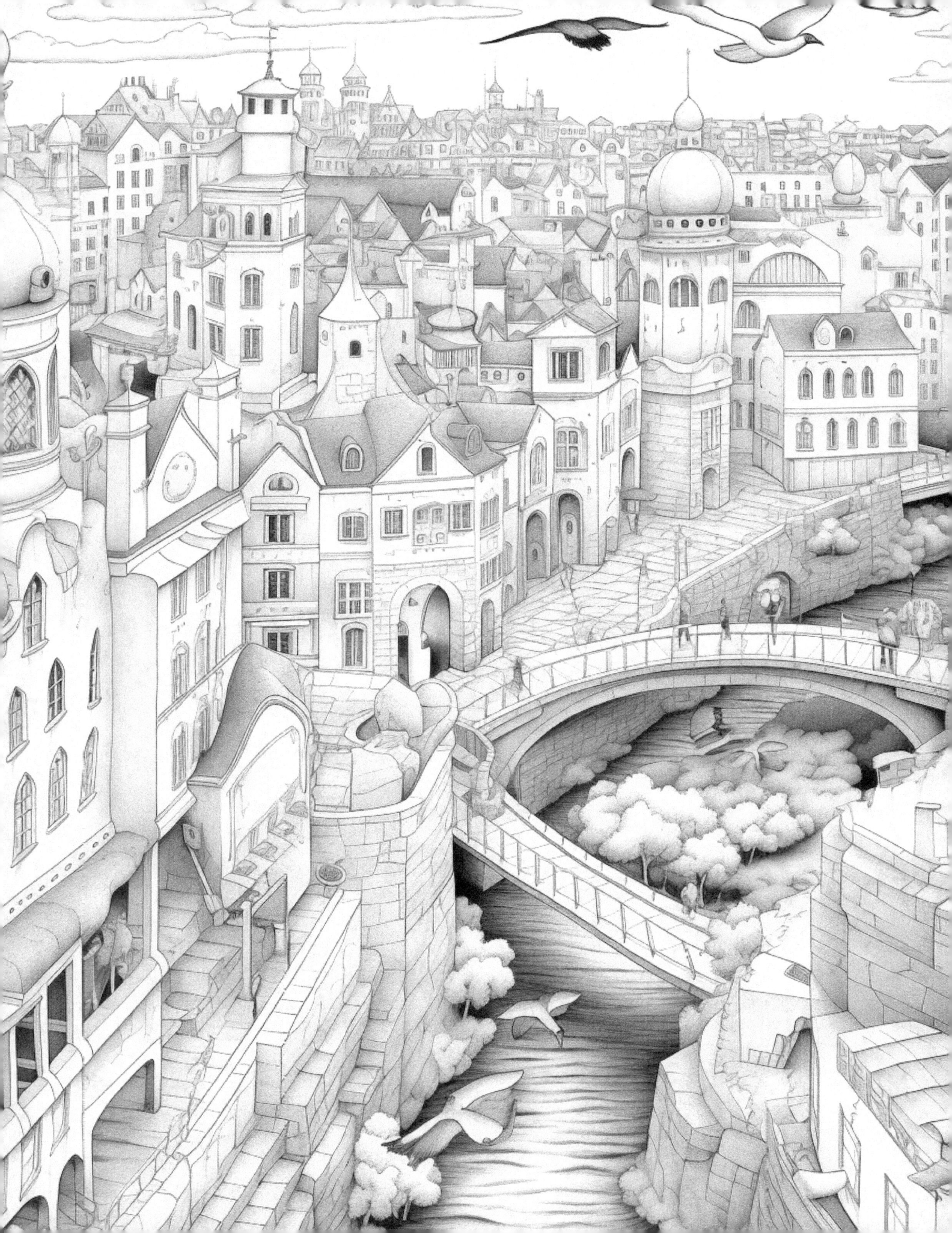

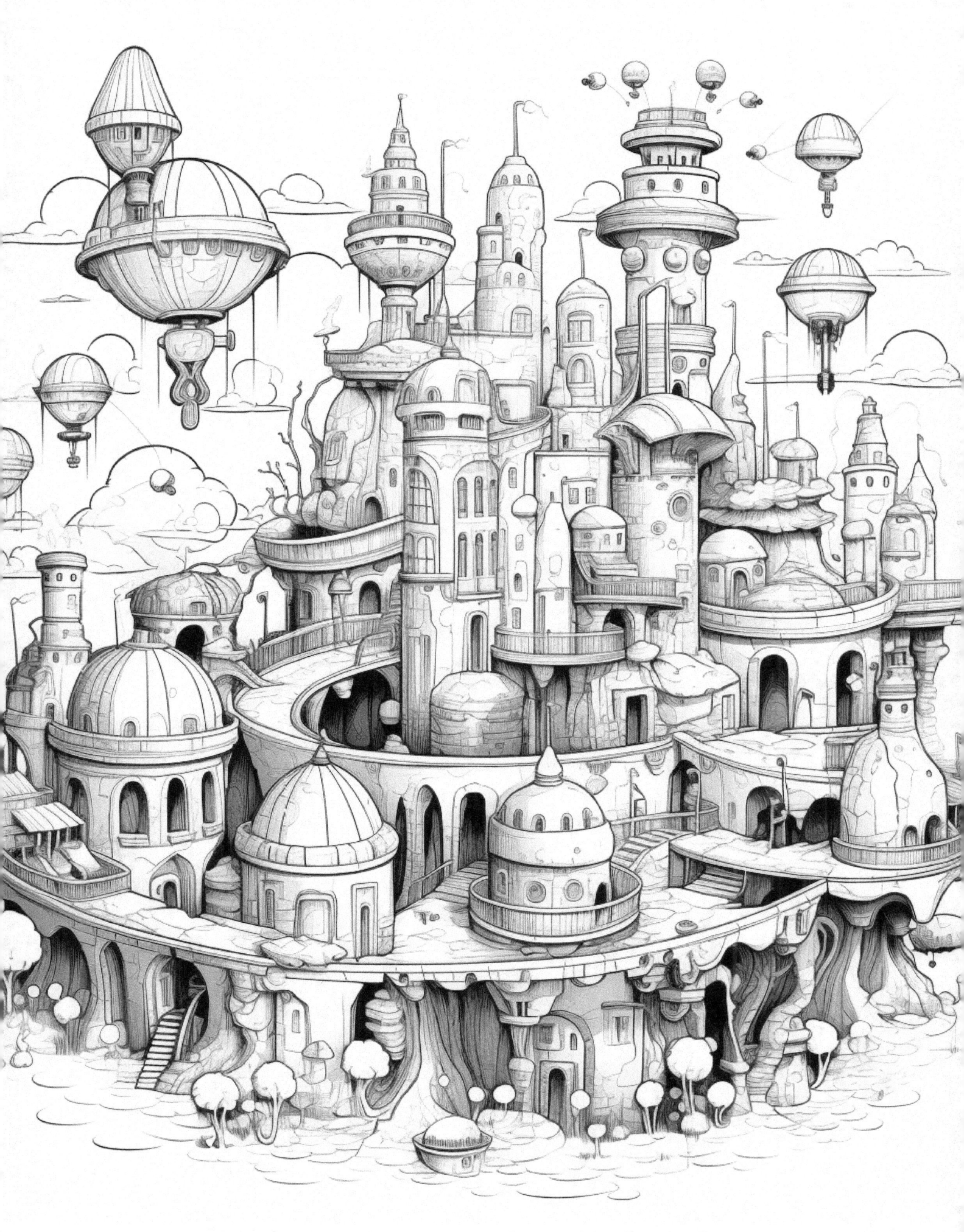

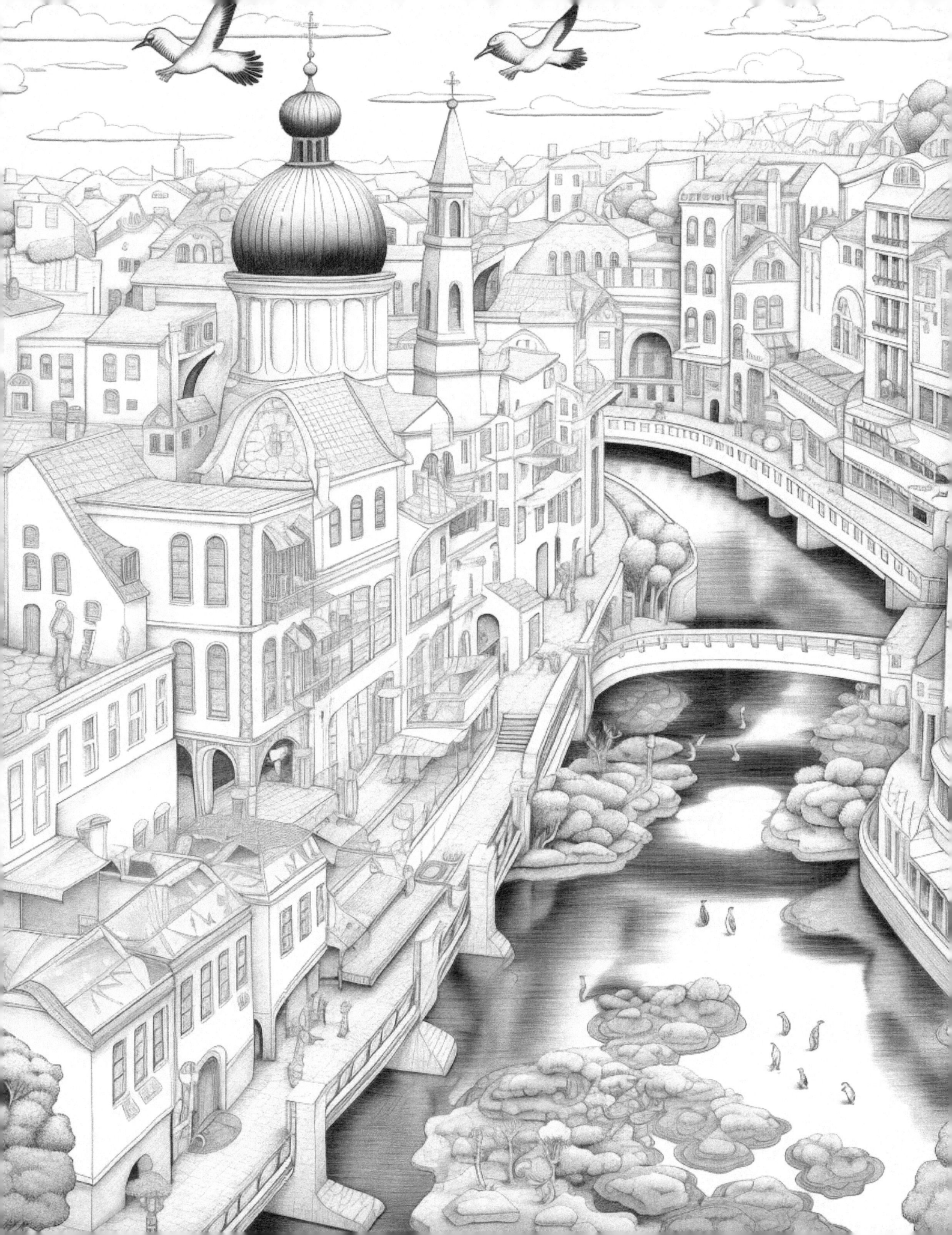

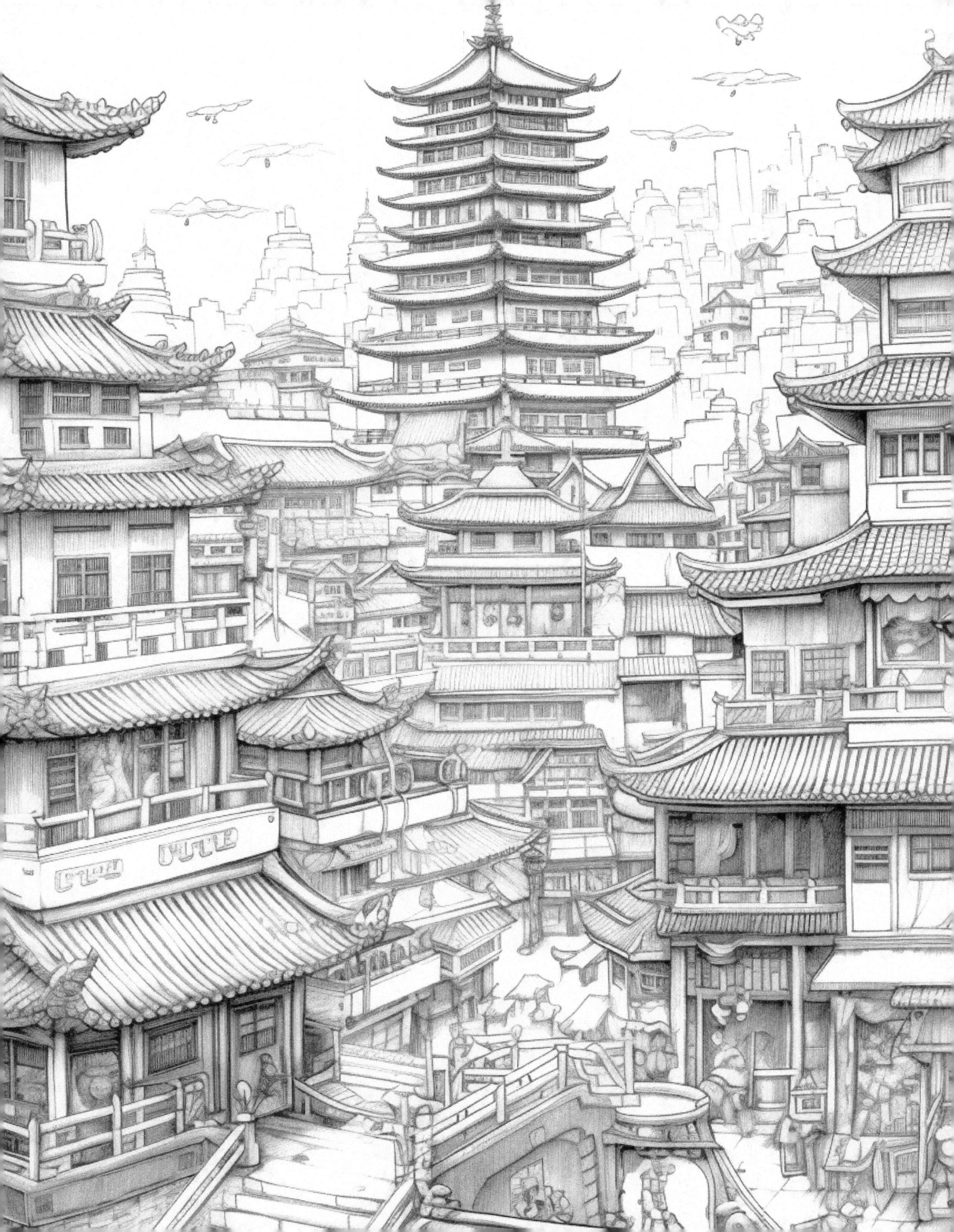

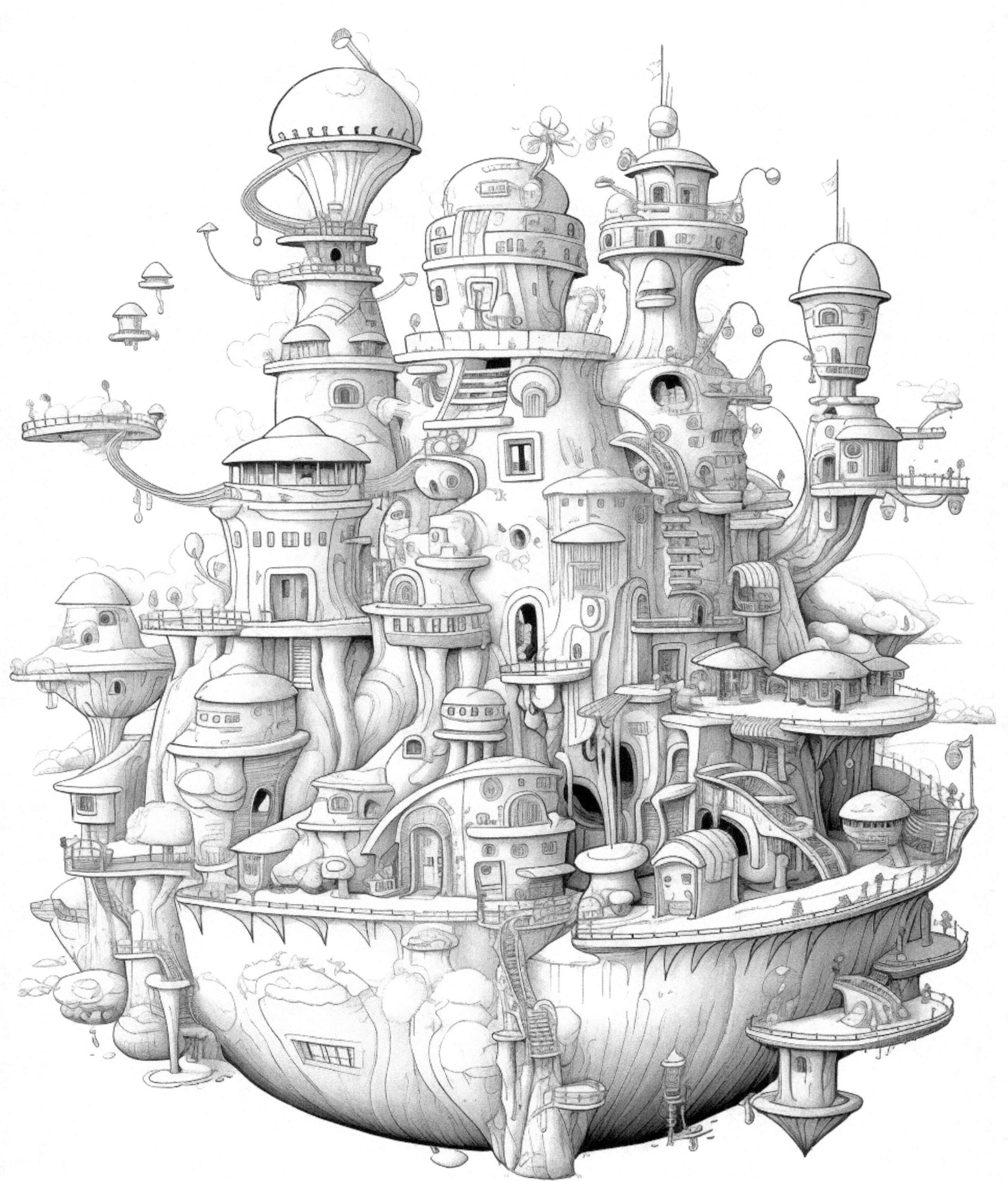

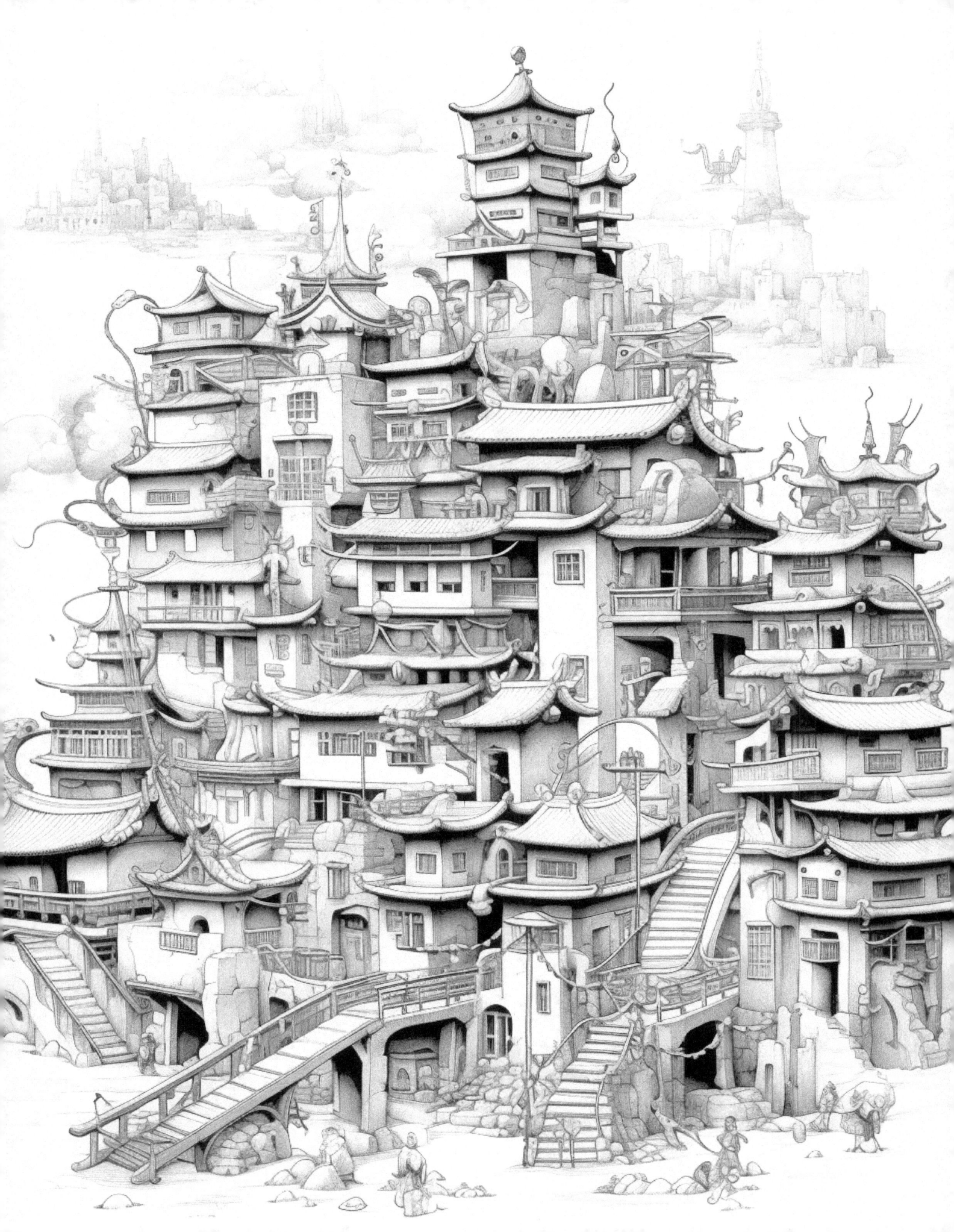

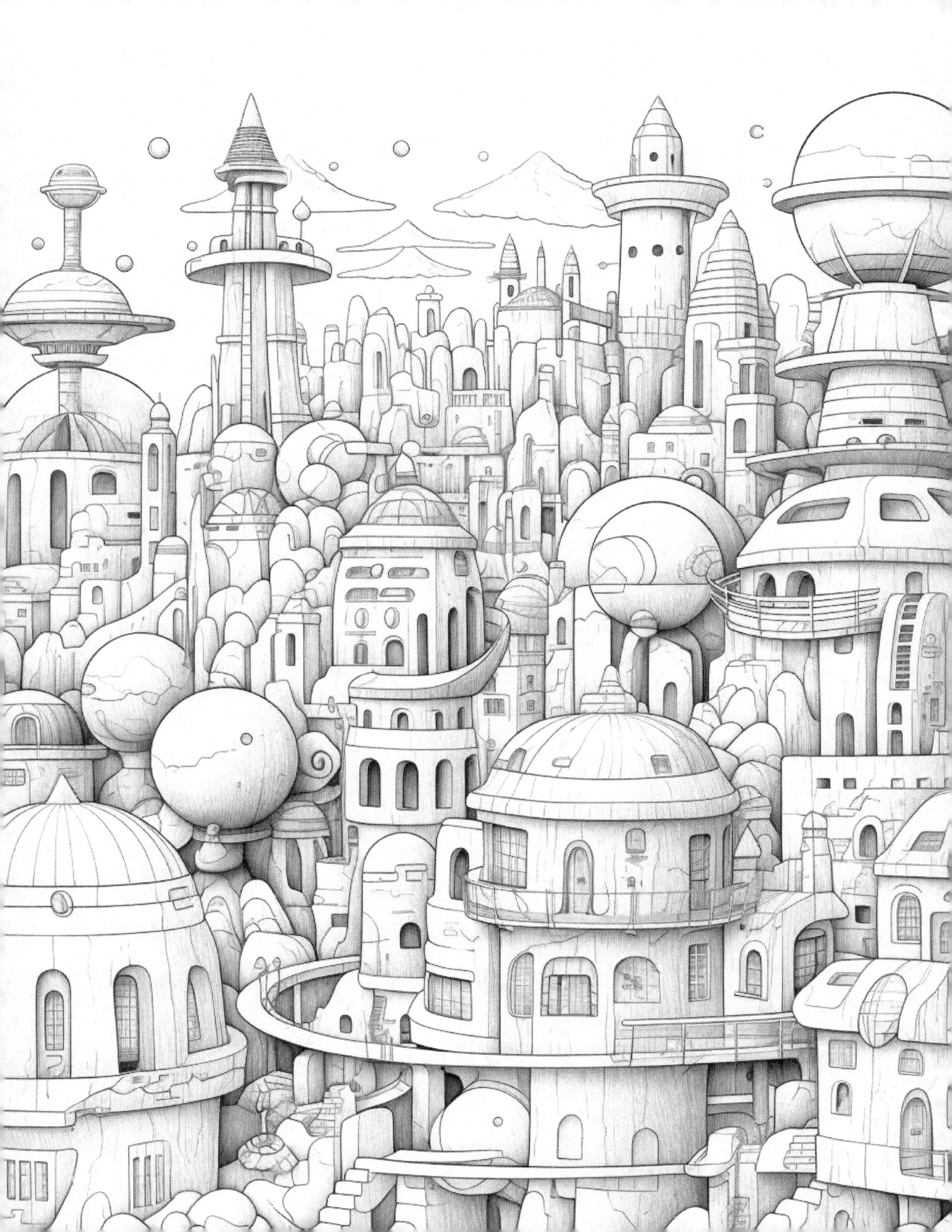

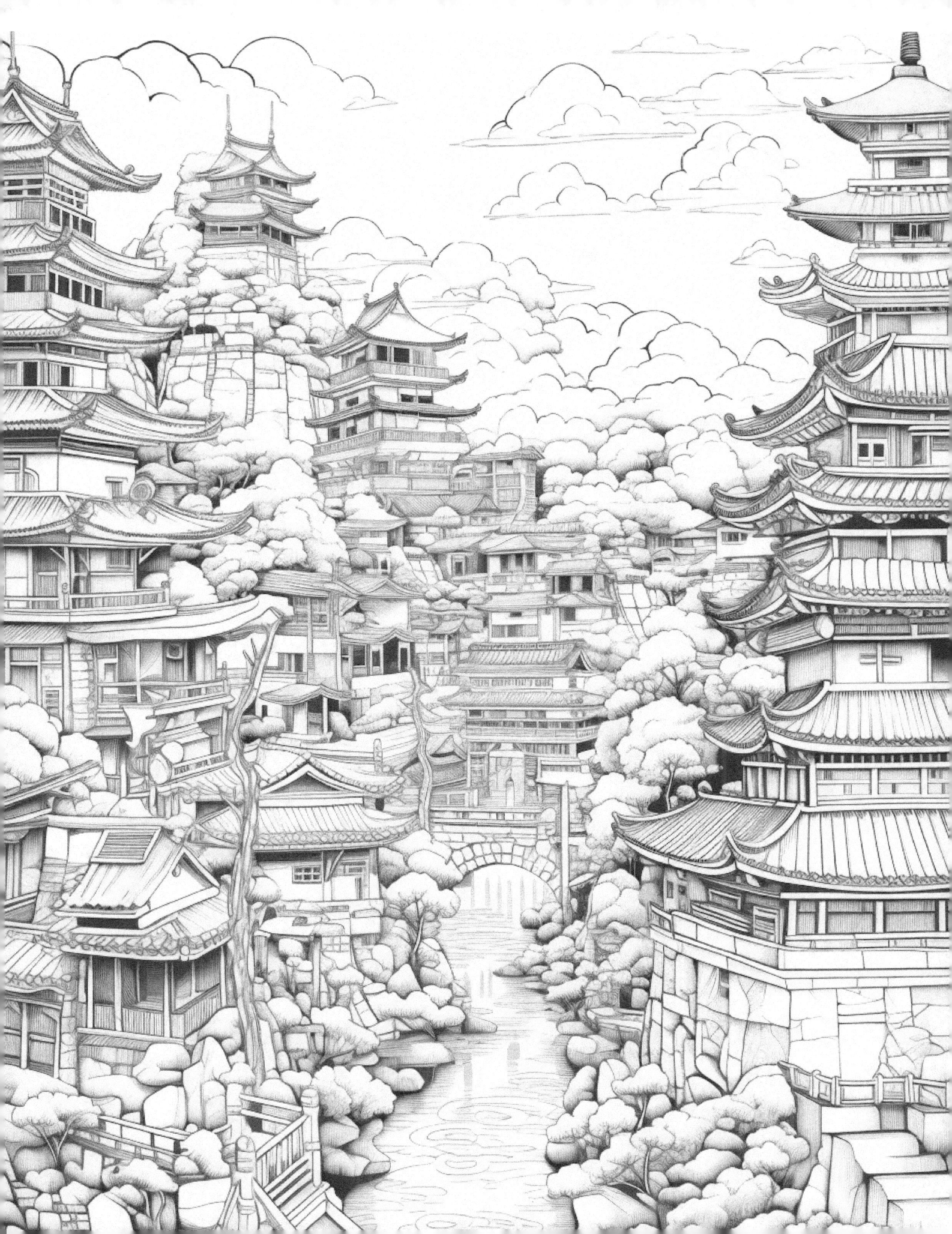

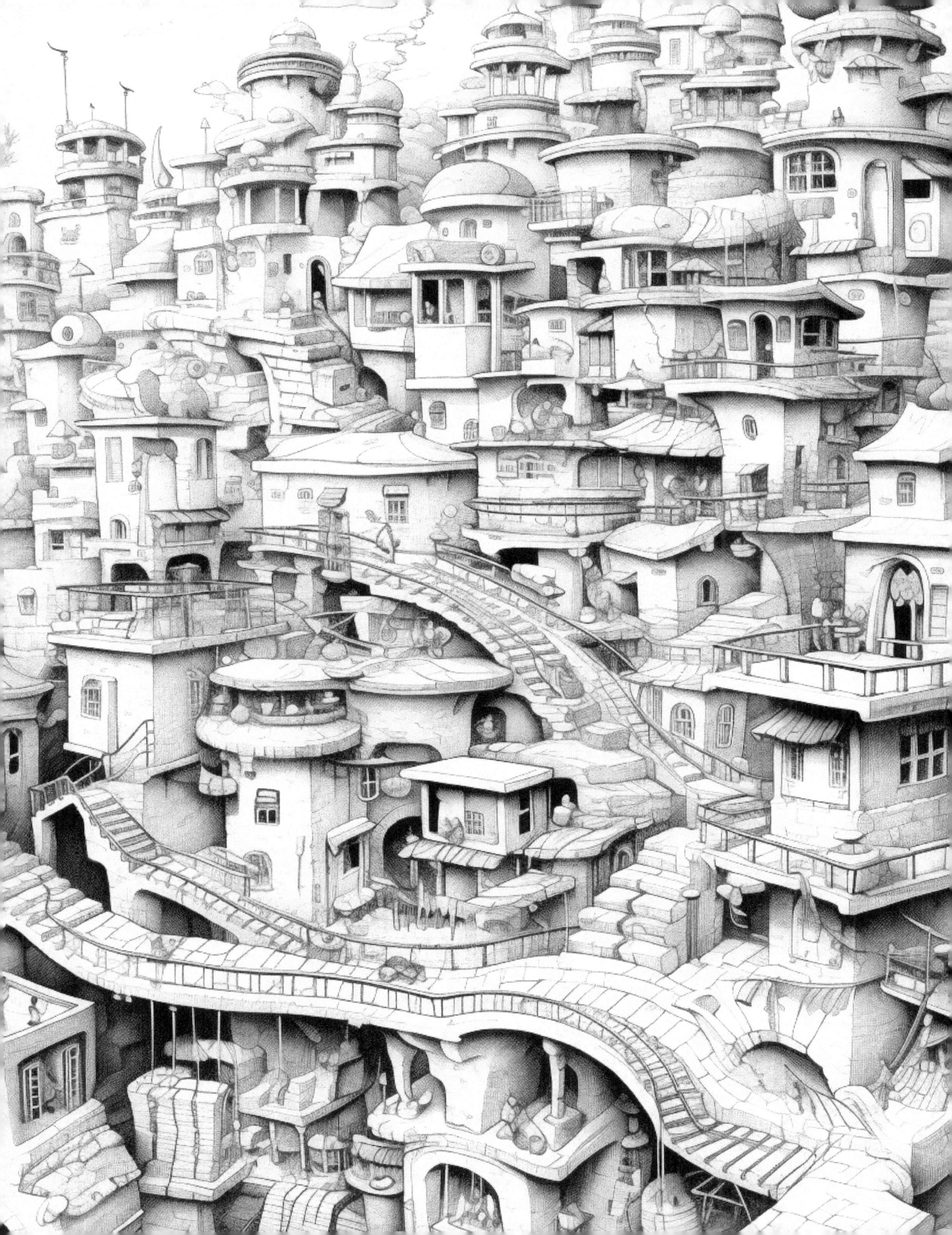

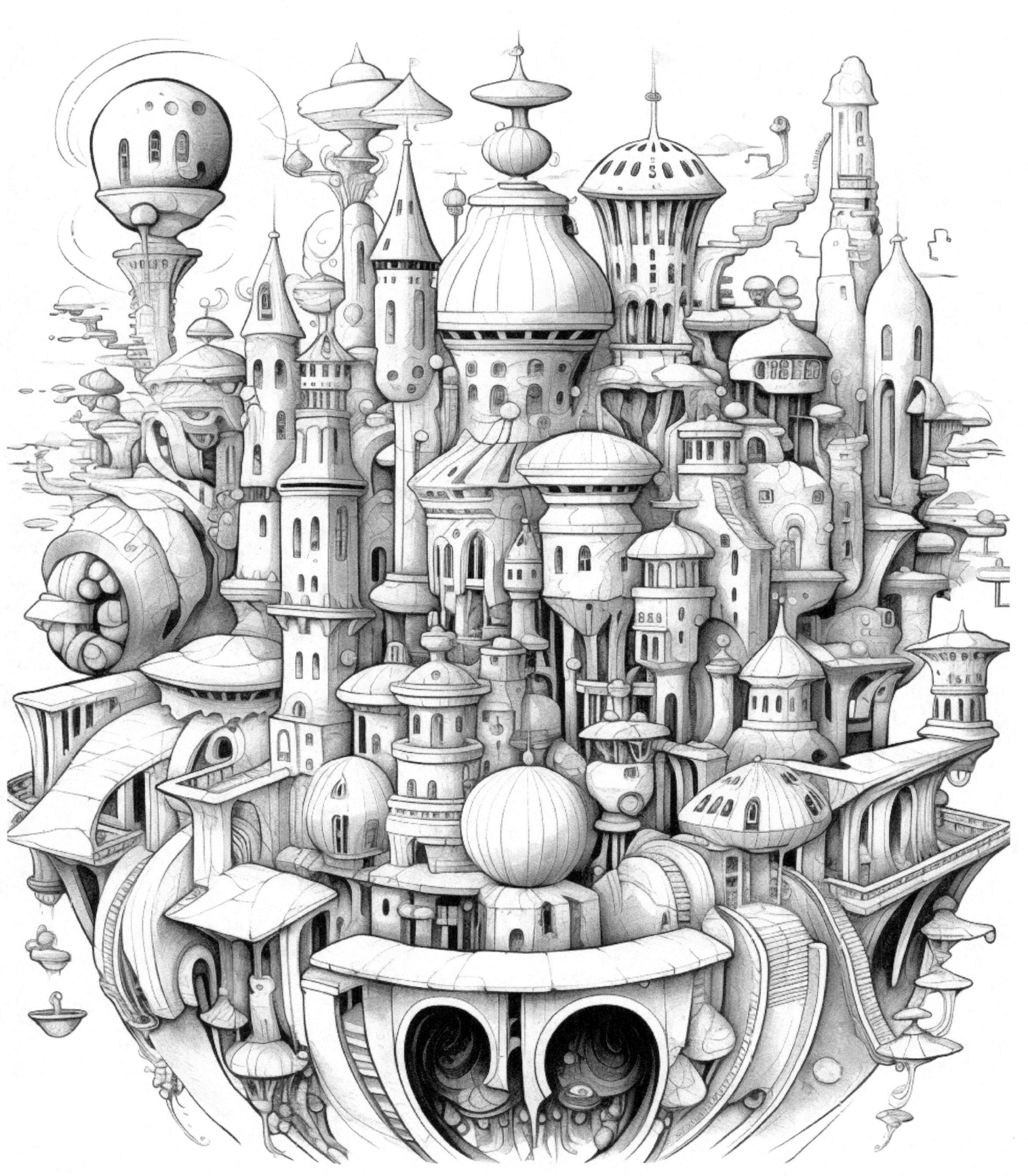

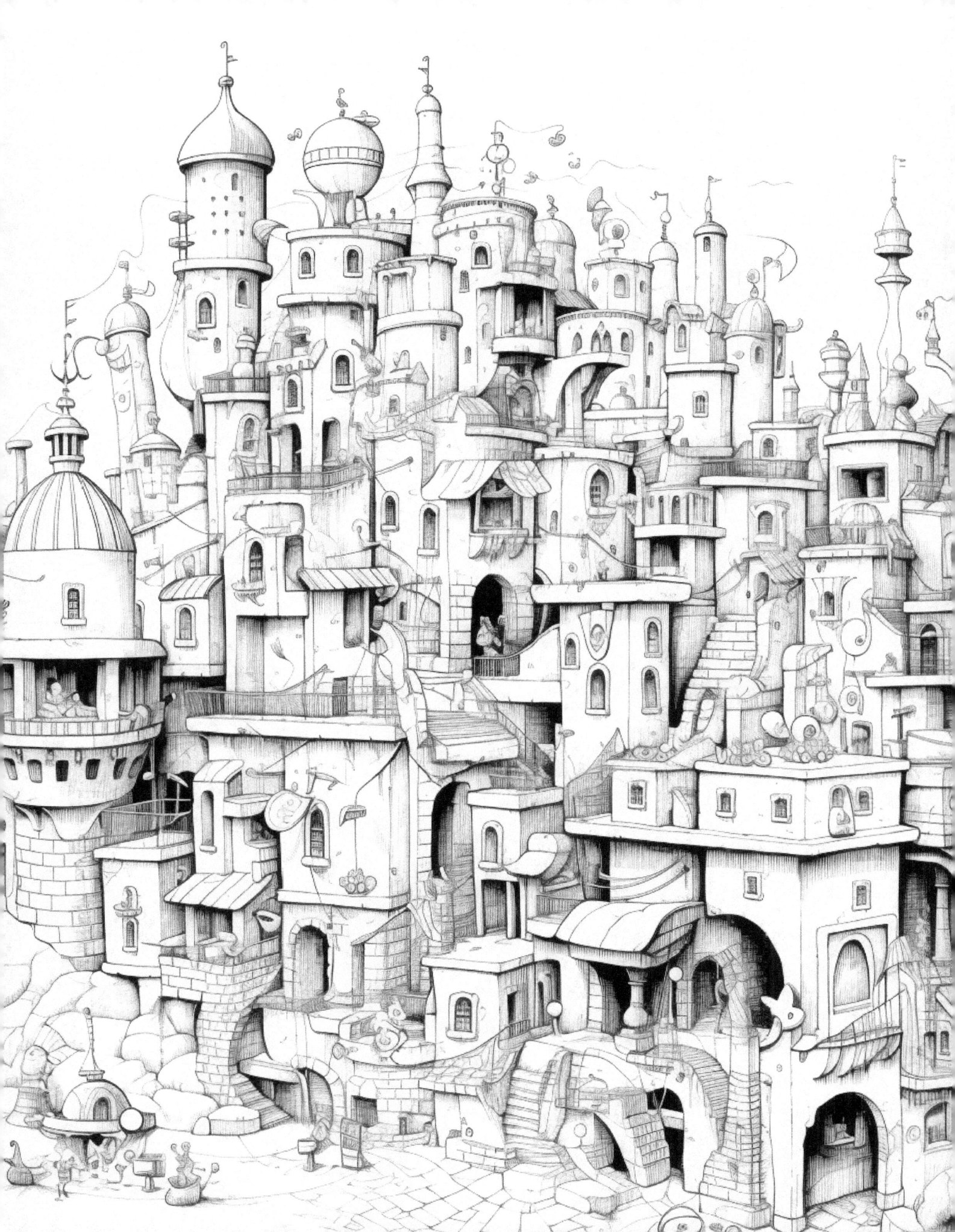

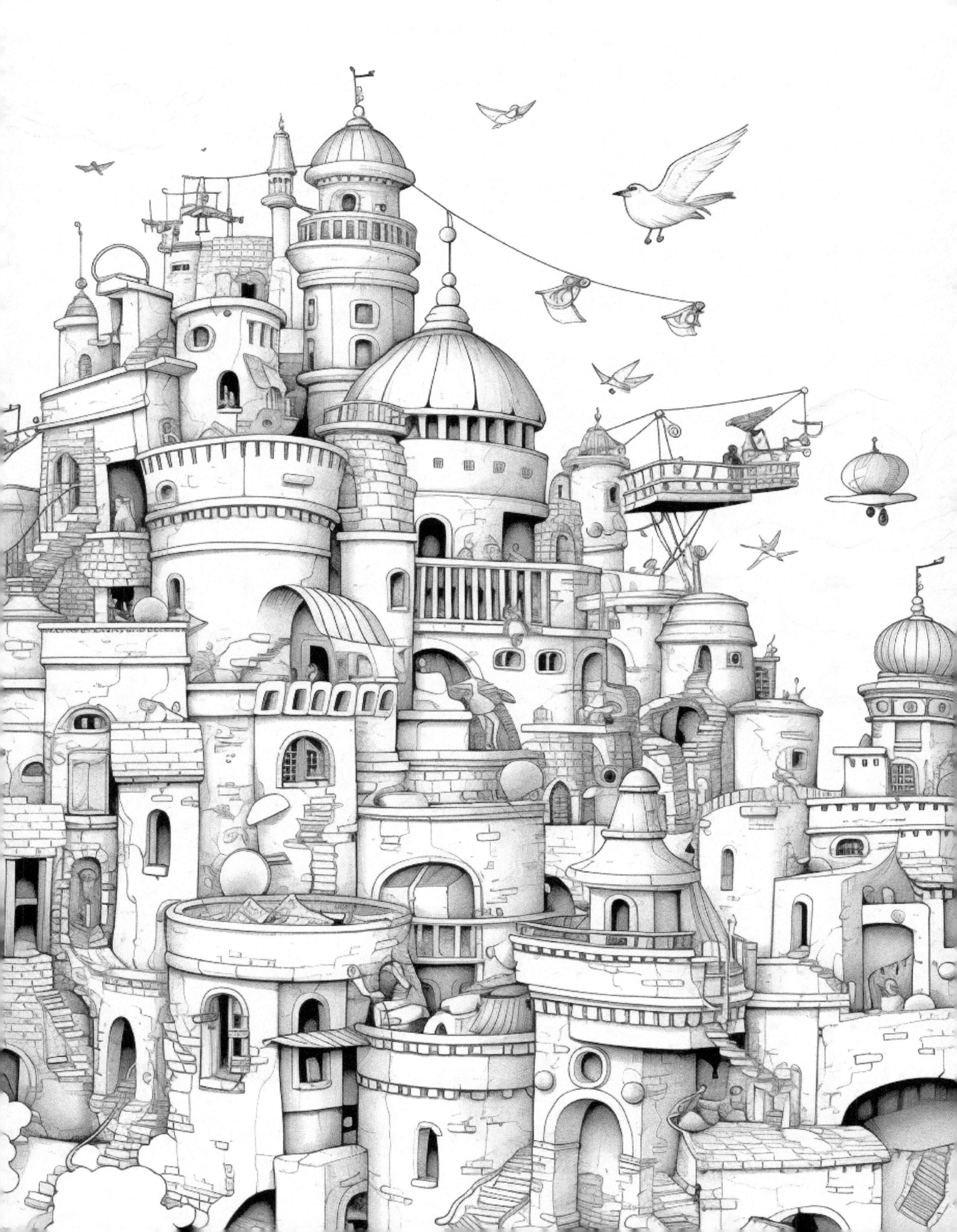

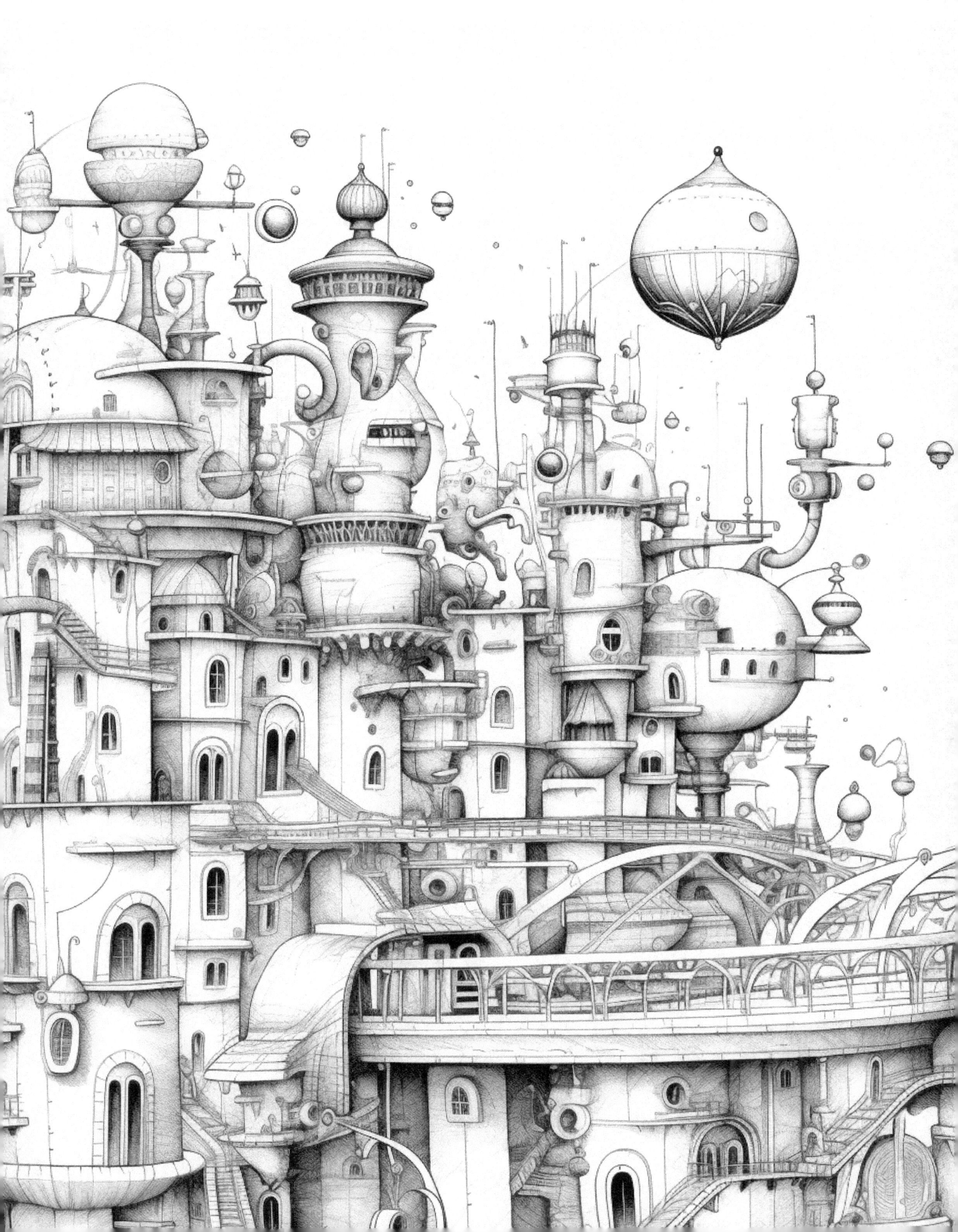

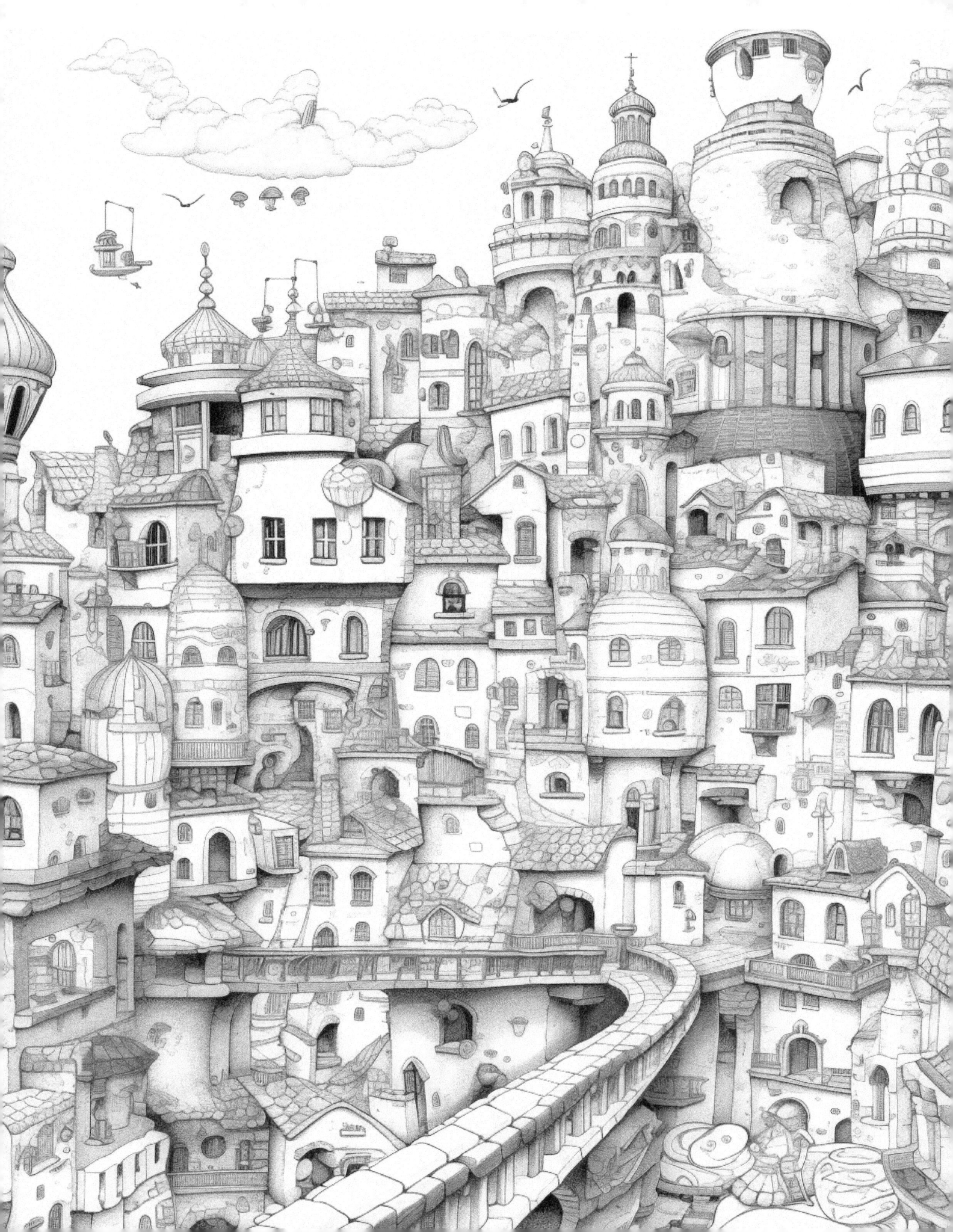

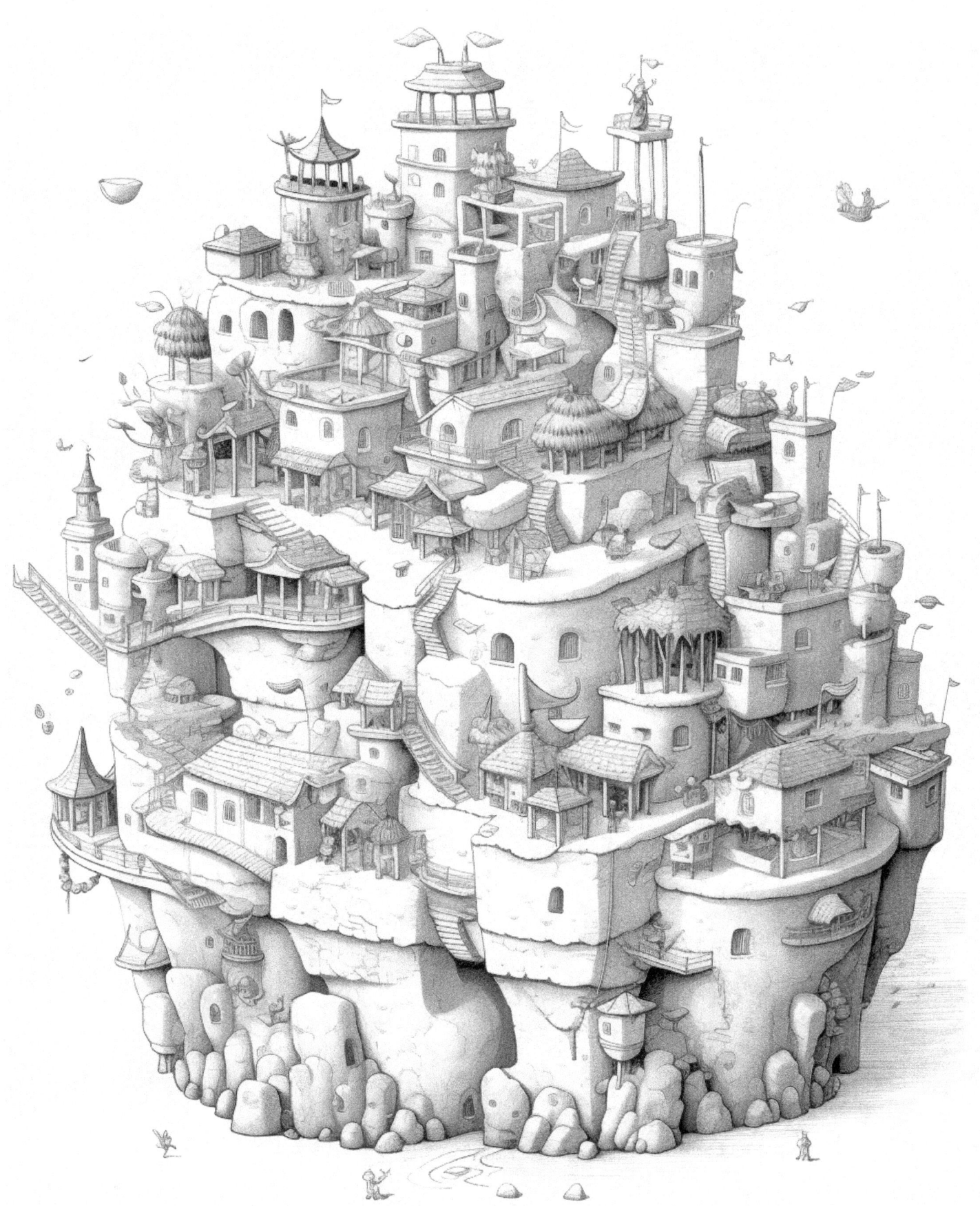

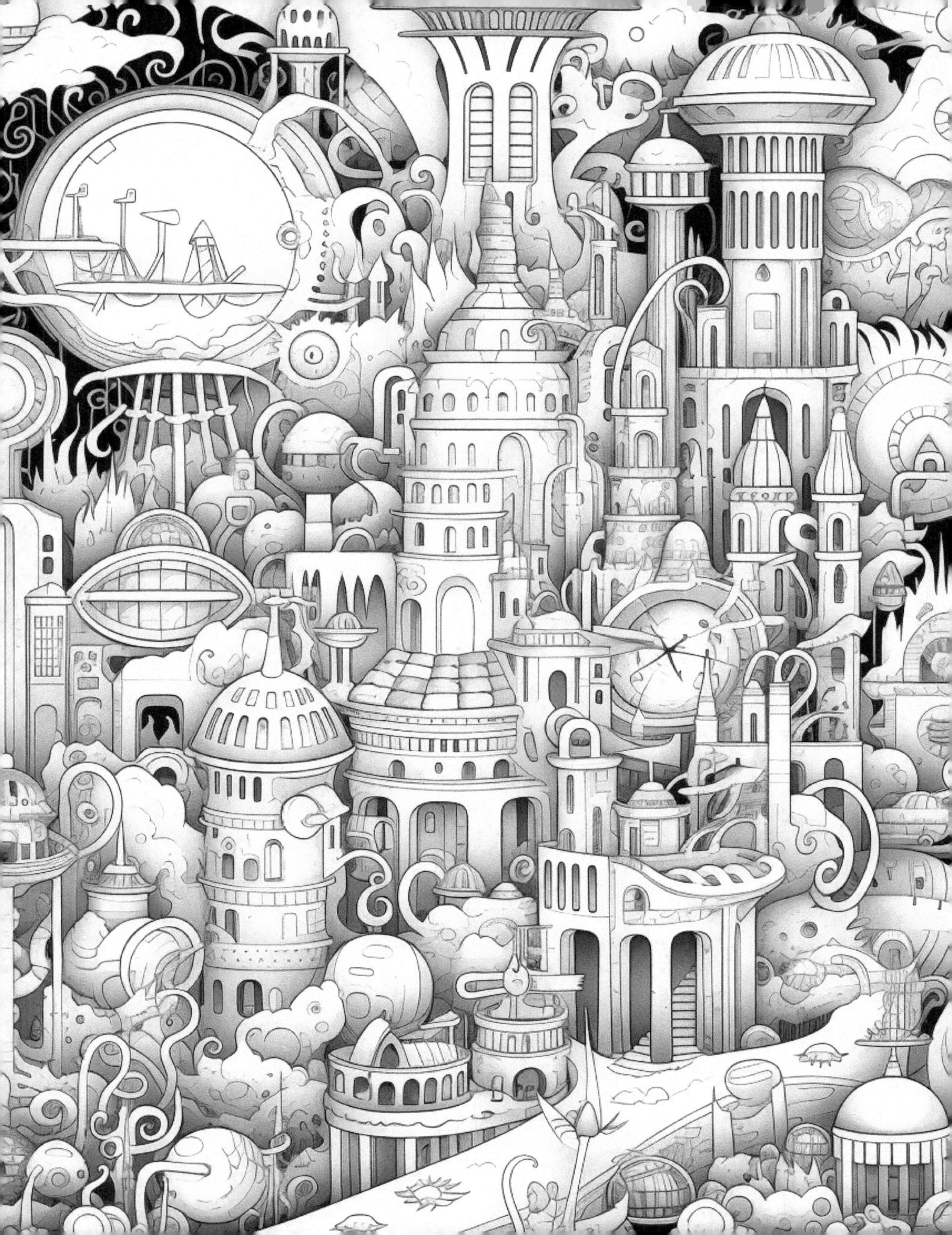

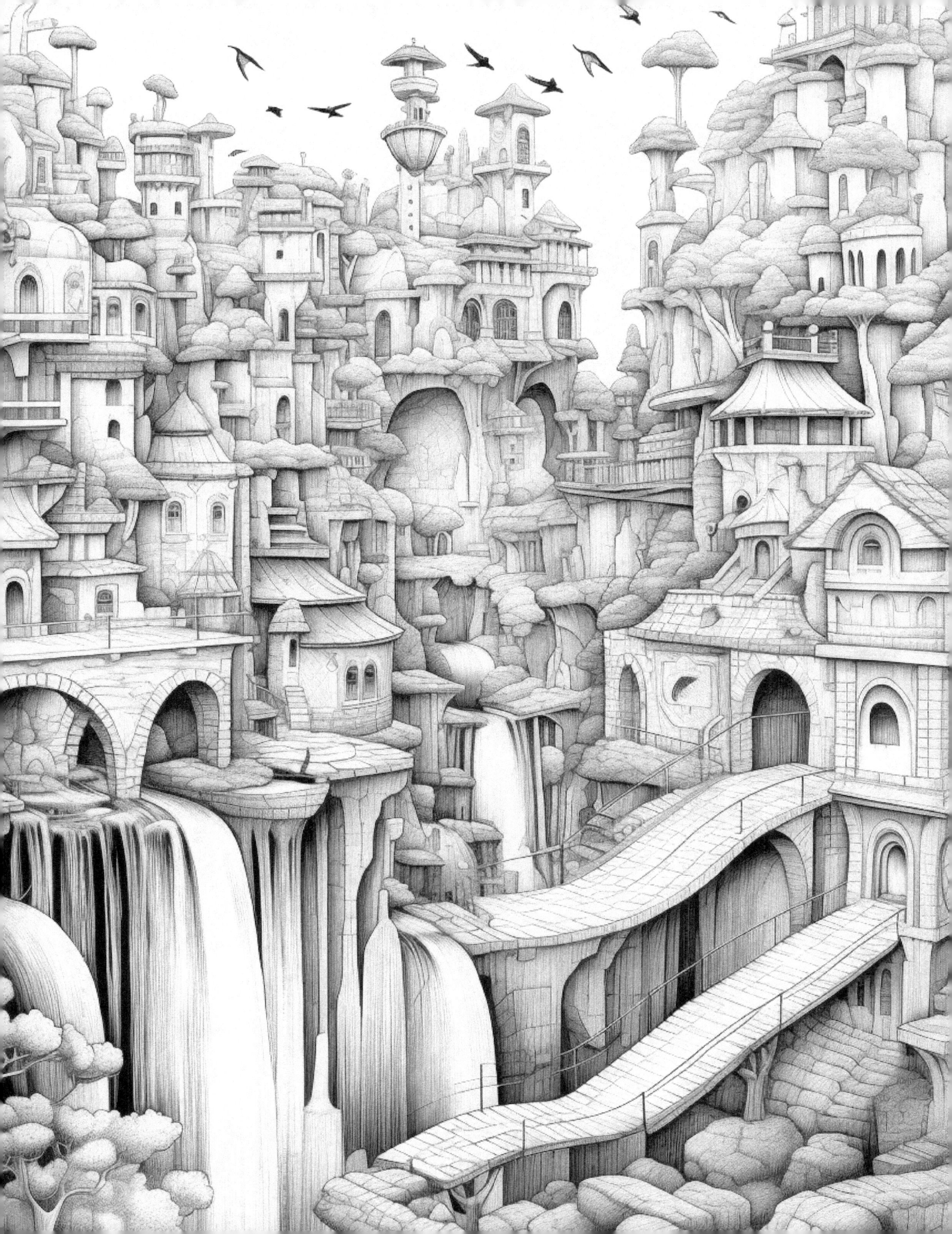

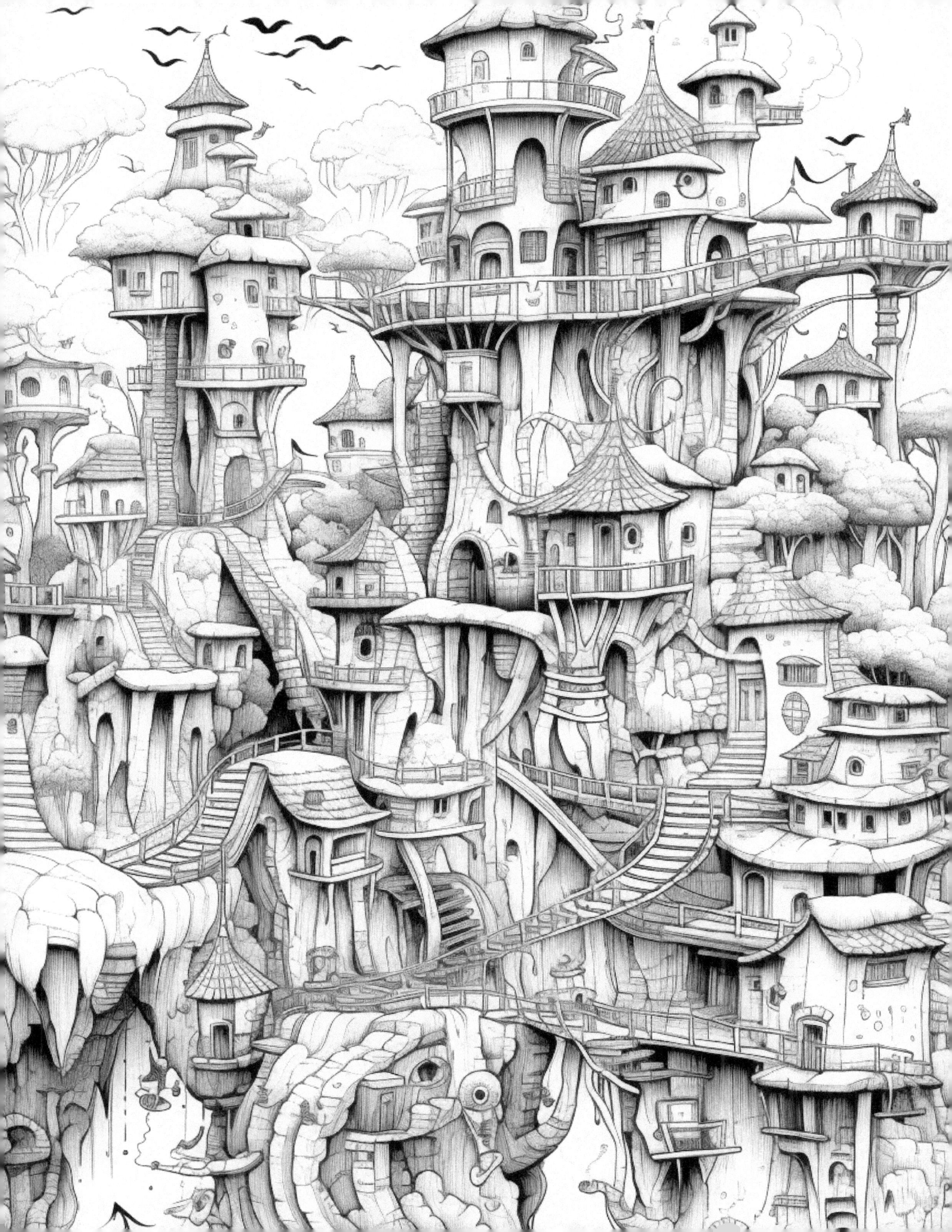

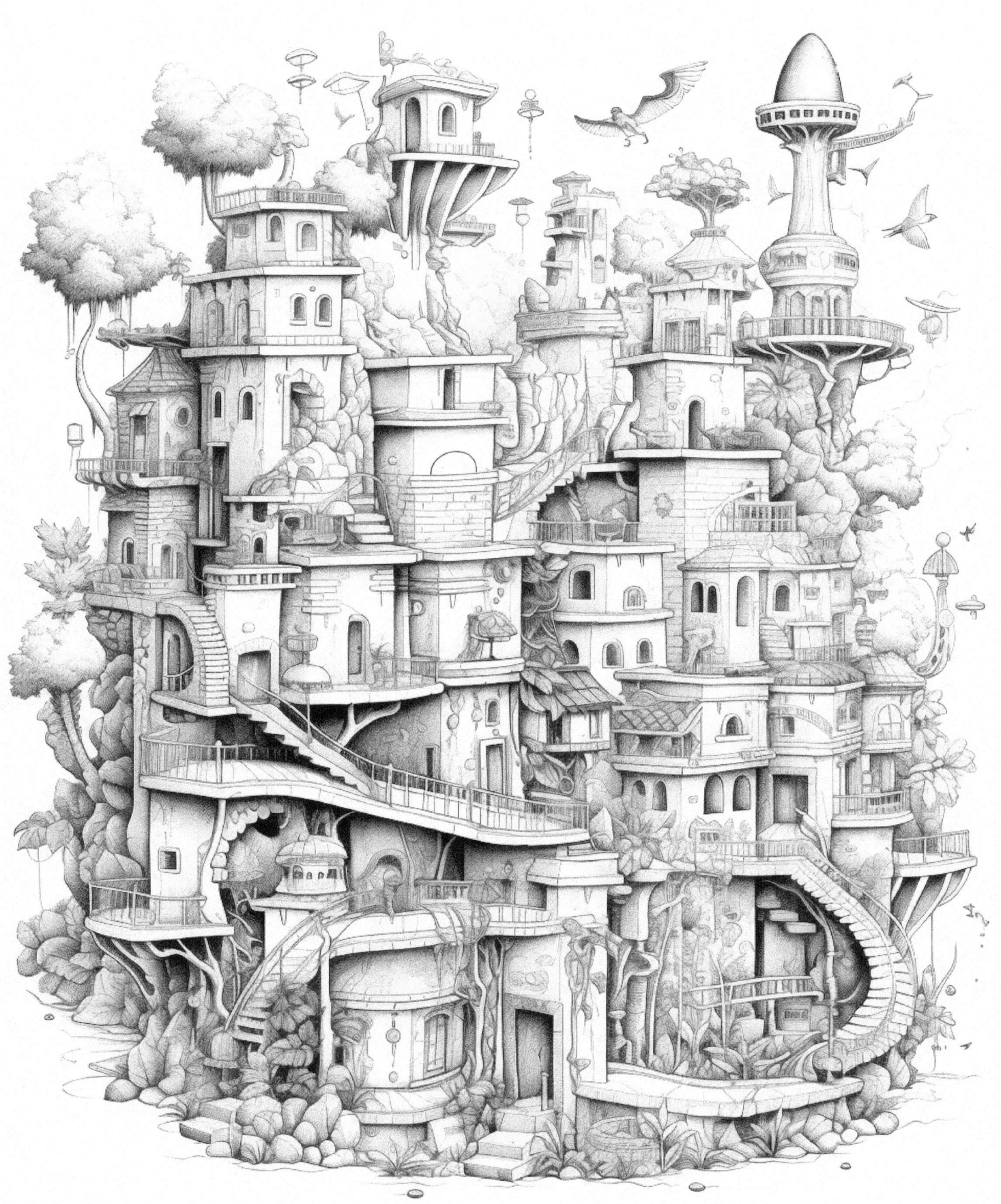

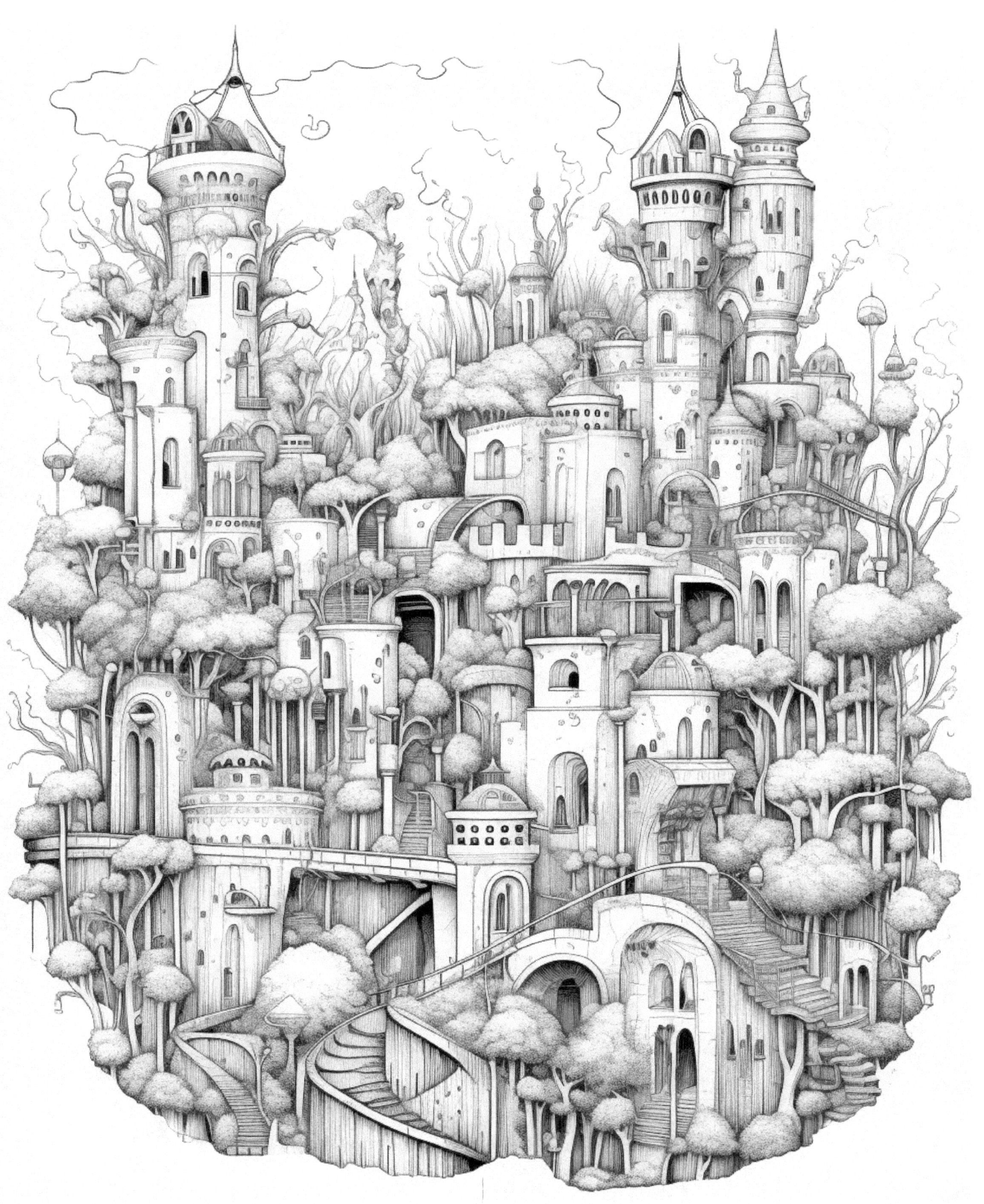

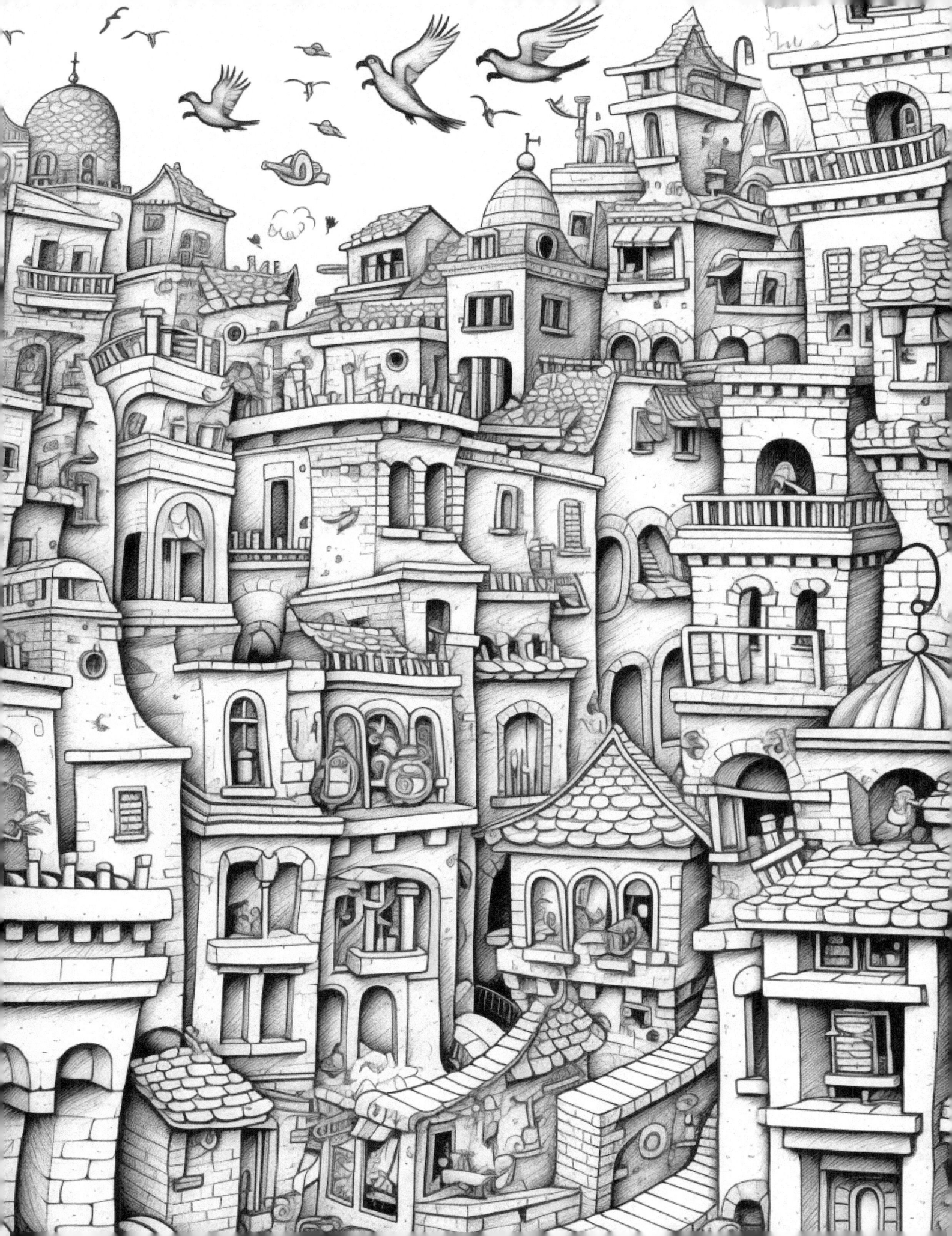

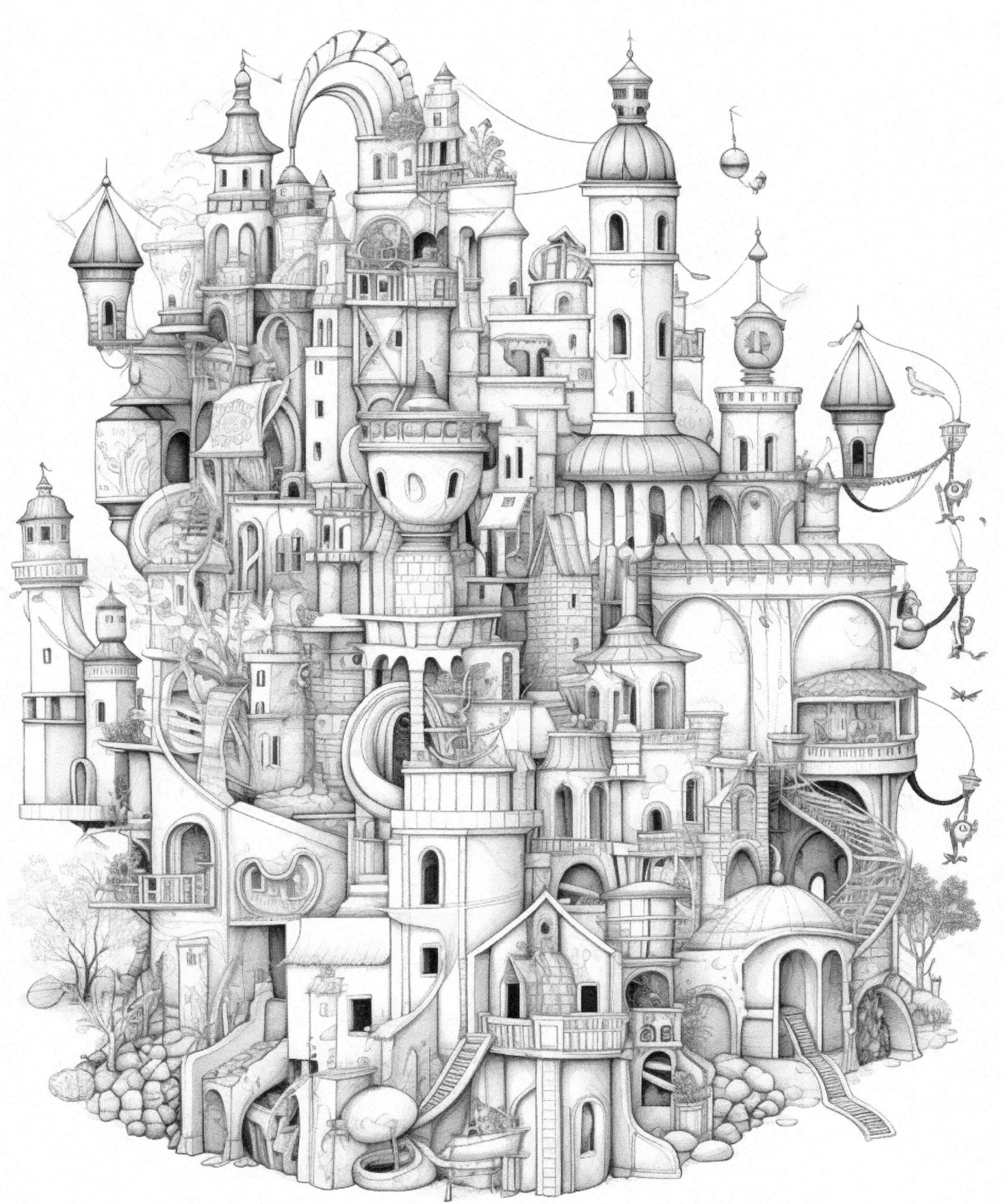

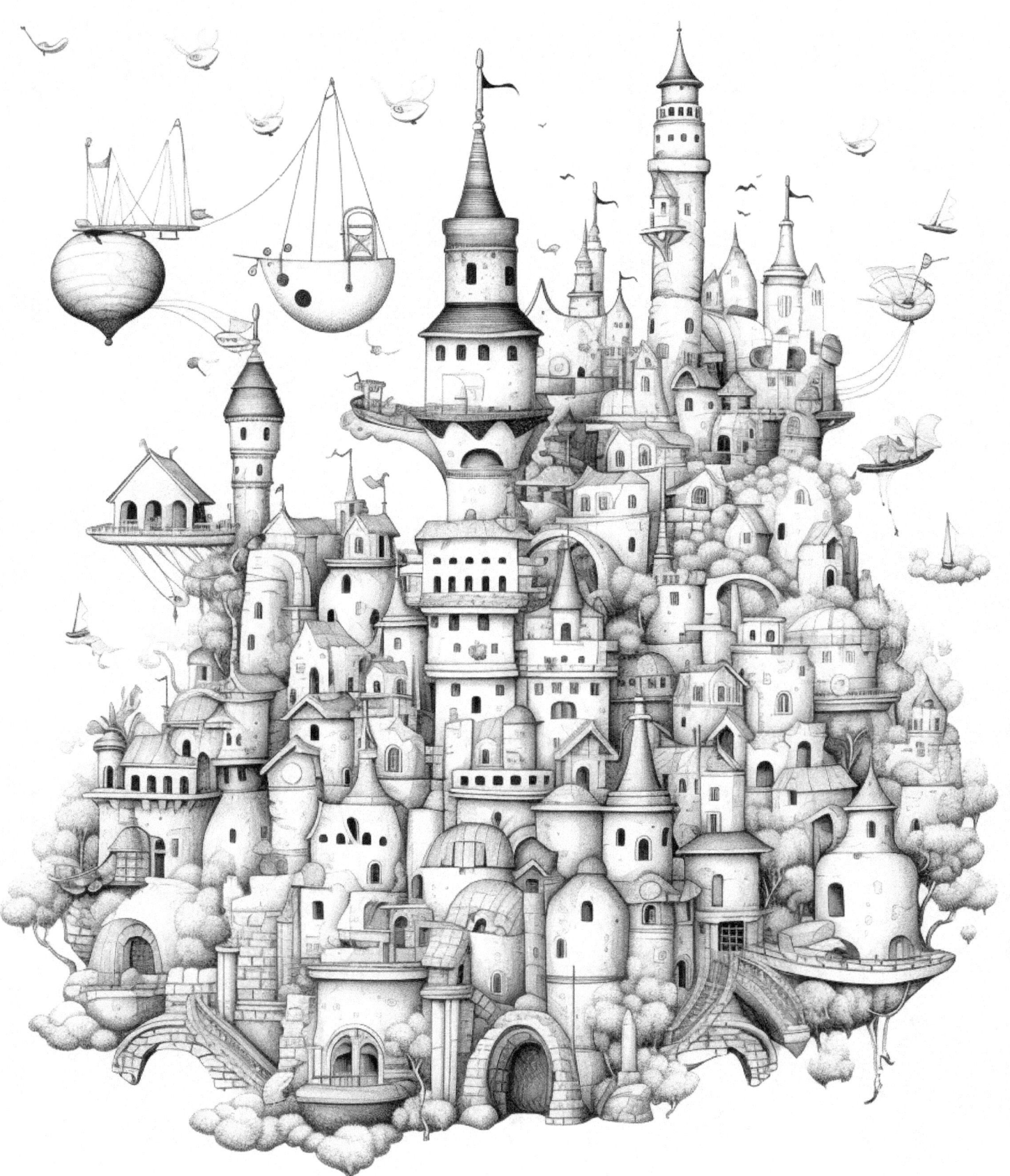

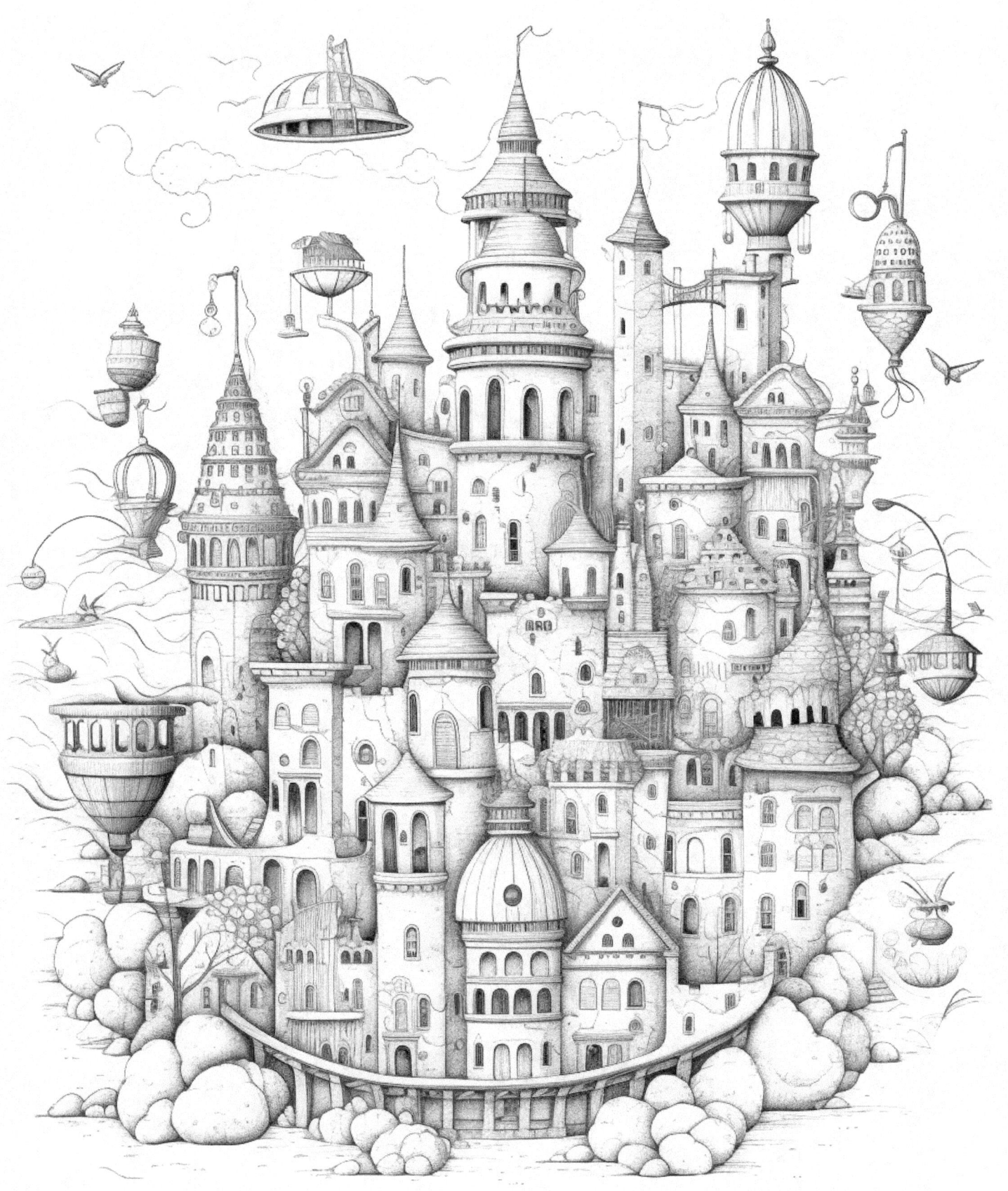

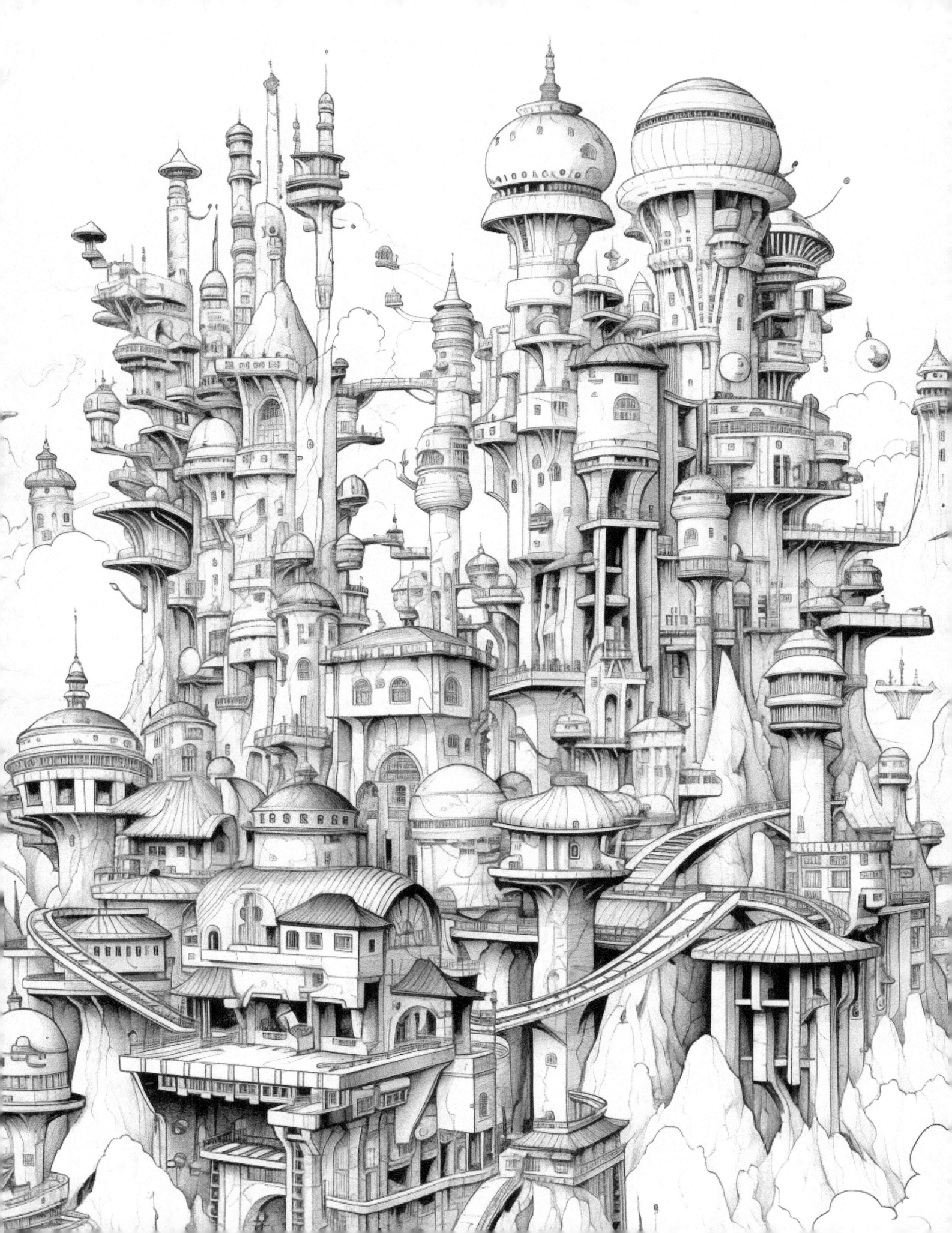

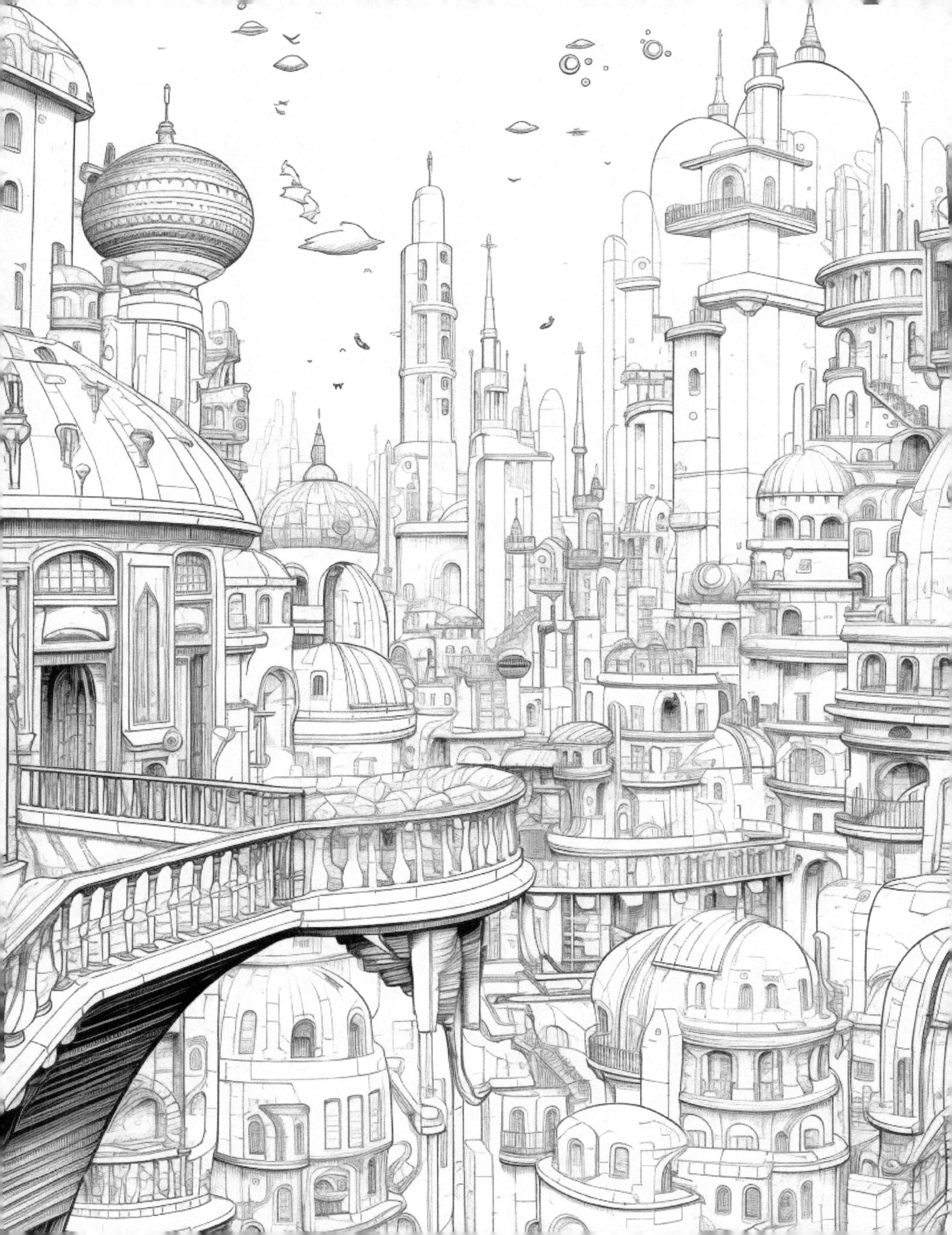

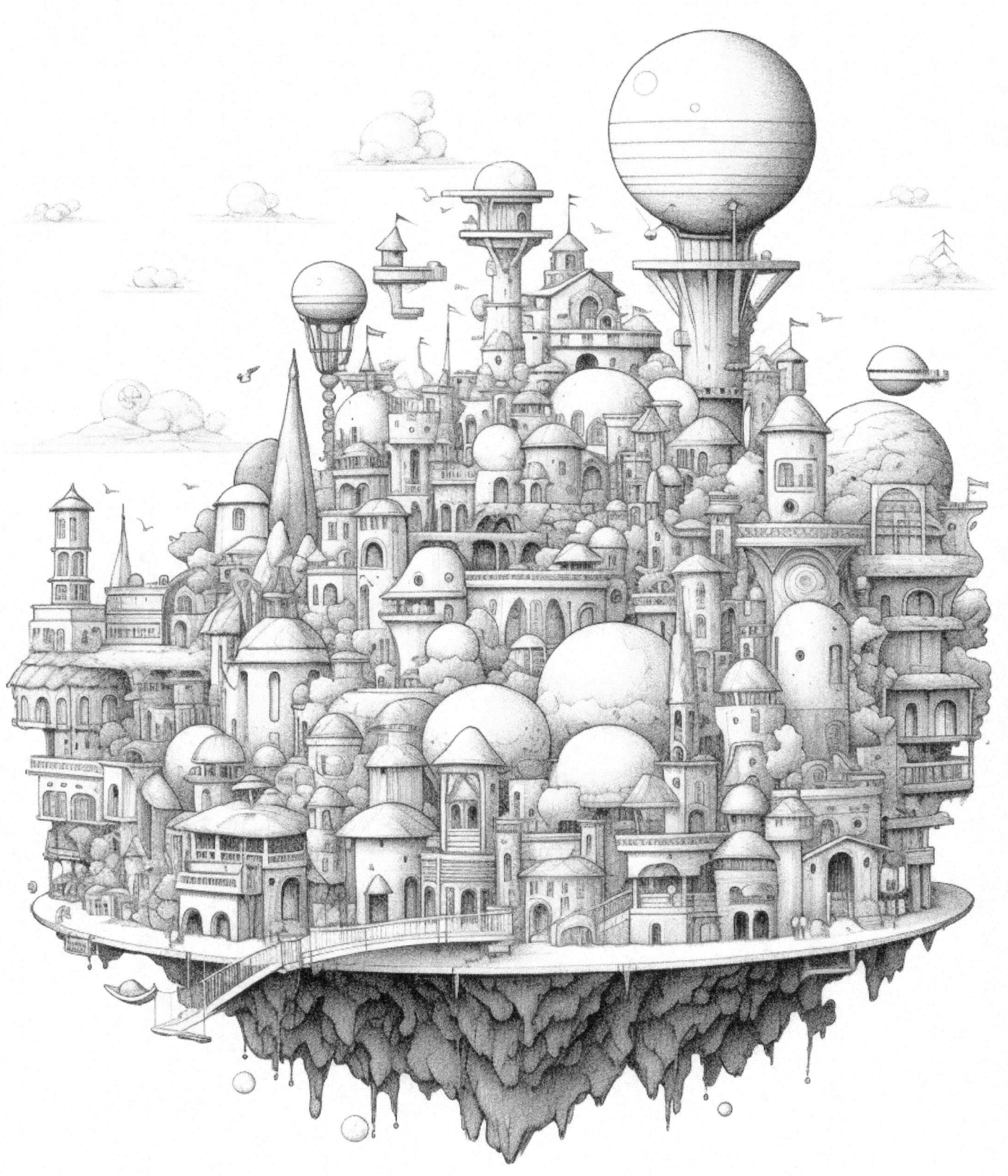

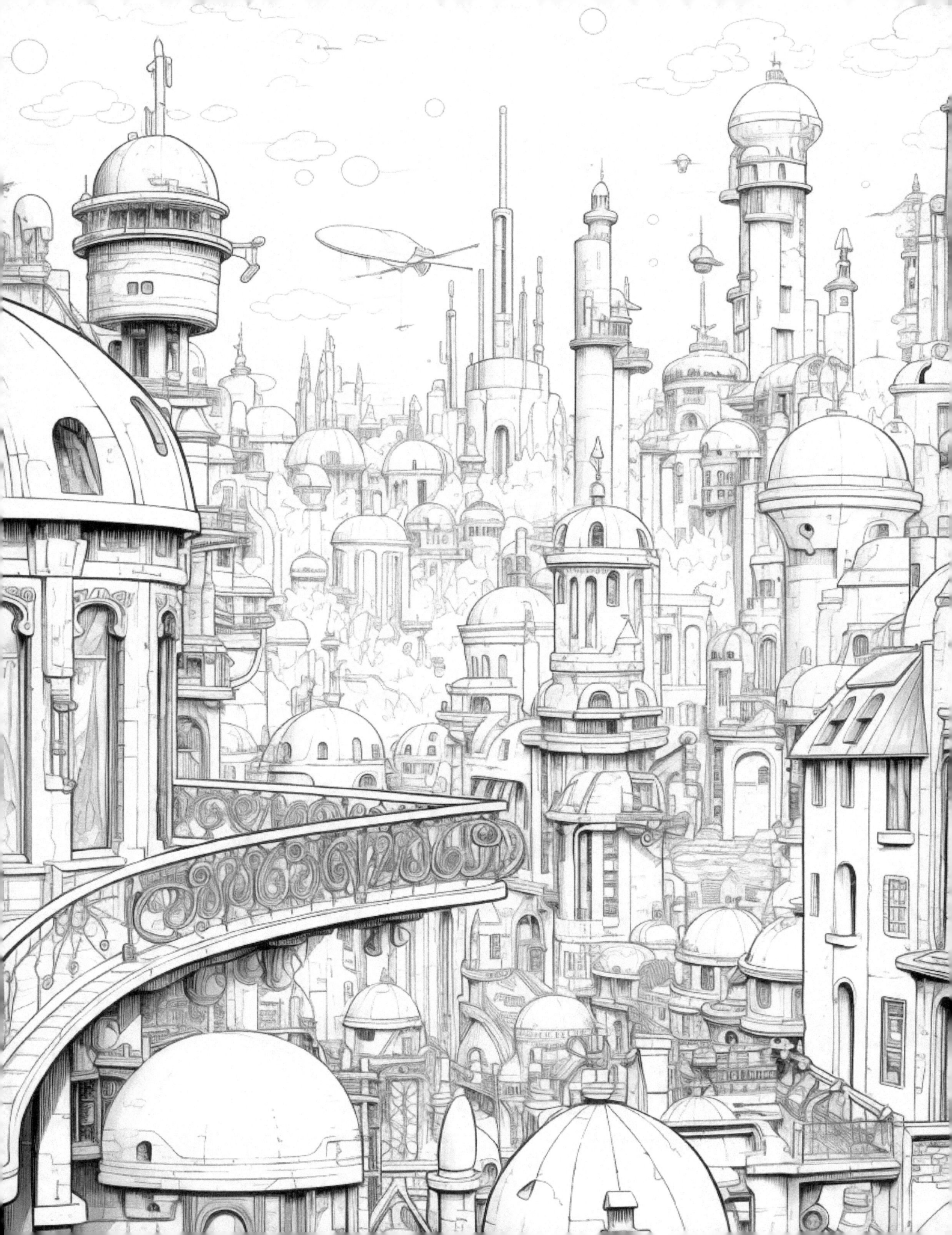

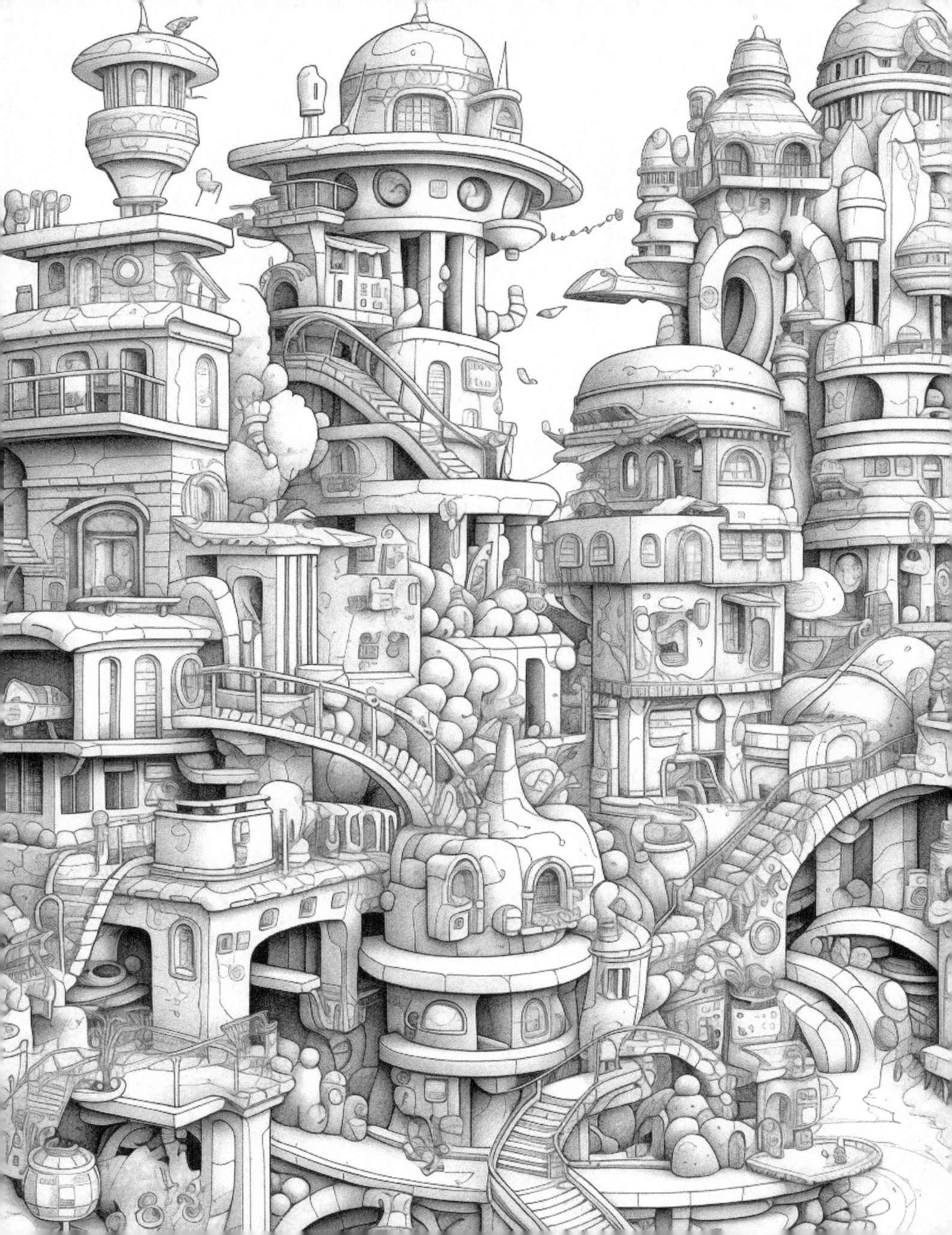